FISHING THE UNEXPECTED

FISHING

the

UNEXPECTED

NAVIGATING *the*

UNPREDICTABLE WATERS

of ENTREPRENEURSHIP

ALEJANDRO MESA

HOUNDSTOOTH
PRESS

FISHING THE UNEXPECTED
Navigating the Unpredictable Waters of Entrepreneurship

FIRST EDITION

ISBN   978-1-5445-4685-8   *Hardcover*
      978-1-5445-4684-1   *Paperback*
      978-1-5445-4686-5   *Ebook*

For Laura, Mariana, and Isabel

CONTENTS

"My Soul Is In a Hurry"
—Mário de Andrade

I have counted my years and realized that I have less time to live
than I have lived so far. I have more past than future.
I feel like the child who received a box of candies: After devouring the
first ones quickly, he suddenly realizes that there are not many left
and that these should be better appreciated and truly enjoyed.
I don't have time for endless meetings where statutes, rules, processes, and
internal regulations are discussed, knowing that nothing will be achieved.
I no longer have time to endure absurd people who,
despite their age, have not grown up.
I no longer have time to fight mediocrity.
I don't want to participate in conversations where inflated egos parade.
I can't stand manipulators and opportunists.
I am annoyed by envious people who seek to discredit the most capable, in
an attempt to seize their position and steal their talent and success.
My time is too short to discuss headlines. I focus on the essentials,
for my soul is in a hurry—there are not many candies left.
I like to live with very human beings. Humans who can laugh at their
mistakes and who are not terribly conceited by their successes.
Humans who do not feel prematurely designated
and humans who take responsibility.
Humans who defend human dignity and are willing
to defend truth and righteousness.
This is what makes life worthwhile.[1]
I want to surround myself with people who understand how to touch
the hearts of others. People who have learned through the hard
knocks of life to grow through tender touches of the soul.
Yes, indeed—I am in a hurry. I am in a hurry to live with the
intensity that only maturity can offer. I try not to waste
any of the sweets that are still left. I am sure they will be
even more delicious than those I have already enjoyed.
My goal is to reach the end—content. At peace with
myself, my loved ones, and my Conscience.

---

1   Mário de Andrade, "My Soul Is In a Hurry," commonly misattributed. Original author likely Ricardo Gondim Rodrigues.

INTRODUCTION

In 2008, while the United States' economy was collapsing and the world was plunging headlong into a recession, I was invited to a cocktail party hosted by a porcine-genetics company that had just turned fifteen years old. I had just returned to Colombia after living in the US for nine years, and I found the celebratory atmosphere in Medellín disorienting. But that party sticks in my memory not because it was a particularly memorable celebration but because that is when I had a conversation that led to the worst business decision of my life.

Piscícola El Rosario, the aquaculture business that came out of that cocktail party, amassed millions in debt in the ten years it operated. By the time it was liquidated, I had lost money, friends, and focus. I beat myself up for years, wondering how I could have been part of such a failure when I—and my partners—had successfully run other businesses. Why was the fish farm alone a black hole, seemingly designed to absorb capital?

If you have ever had to liquidate a business or are currently struggling to keep one afloat, you probably understand how easy it is to cast blame or wallow in guilt. I found myself in that boat until I attended an event run by Dan Sullivan, the co-founder of Strategic Coach®, and did a simple exercise called "The Experience Transformer."

The exercise begins with the recognition that any experience of certain dimensions has significant value, regardless of whether it has been a success or a failure. Sullivan suggests that what we consider a failure—a bankruptcy, a failed strategy, a falling out among partners—is a very important asset. The exercise is about documenting what worked and what did not, as well as imagining how we would do things differently if we had them to do over again. The expectation is that these learnings multiply your knowledge, enabling you to do things faster, better, and at less cost in the future.

So, in spite of the bad taste in my mouth over what I had lost in the aquaculture business, I began to connect the dots. During the two years between the liquidation of the company and the arrival of the pandemic, I scribbled notes on airline napkins, finally able to look fearlessly at the company's largest problems when the world looked so small below me. Those notes about the honors and horrors of running a business became the basis of this book.

WHO I AM

In 1979, when I was five years old, my father founded Premex, a company that produces premixed animal feed components. As a child, I spent all my free time at the factory, drowning the workers in questions and soaking up my father's interactions with customers. Many people, upon seeing my interest, would put a hand on my head and say something like, "Here's the future head of the business."

As an adult, I studied agronomy at Zamorano University in Honduras, taking courses like "Statistics" and "Goats and

Sheep" and working in the university's ten thousand acres of gardens and processing plants. I then underwent a second undergraduate program in the United States, joined a chemical additive company in Medellín, served as an executive at a pharmaceutical company in New York, and headed Premex's international expansion from an office in Florida. But nothing compares to what I learned from heading El Rosario. I may not have earned a doctoral degree, but I have earned the equivalent through the dozens of mistakes I made and continue to make as an entrepreneur.

Robert Steven Kaplan, one of the professors I most admired in business school, said that all of us have three stories: the basic facts (e.g., when we were born, where we went to school, when we fell in love), a success story (e.g., the medals we have won), and a failure narrative (i.e., the painful experiences we generally try to hide). He said that this third story is the most powerful and that those who do not pay attention to it end up stunting their talents and their capacity to create value. So, this book is my failure narrative, the story I would prefer to sweep under the rug but am instead sharing to be of service to others who are creating, running, or consolidating businesses. My hope is that the lessons I have learned will help you avoid the mental traps and errors in judgment that affected me.

WHAT YOU WILL LEARN

If anything defines what it is to be human, it is people's ability to gather around a common goal. Businesses are the best version of that: they transform their teams' energies into solutions that meet others' needs, and they do so while respecting liberty. In the end, customers freely choose or reject the products or services an enterprise offers.

This presents an enormous challenge to those of us who run businesses: if we want to be chosen by the market, we have to provide valuable products or services. However, it is easy to lose ourselves in biases—what we think people want and how we think we should operate—so providing value starts with recognizing our limitations. If we recognize our limitations, we can begin innovating solutions that make a difference; if we do not, we may repeat the maneuvers that cause us to fail again and again.

In this book, I will share my experiences heading El Rosario without revealing the identities of my partners, conscious of the fact that what I remember cannot fully reflect the reality of what happened. I will also share some of my experiences successfully navigating tricky situations with other companies. Through these stories, you will learn to invest in your core area; to recognize companies as biological systems; to optimize group dynamics; to cultivate a growth mindset; to leverage mathematical thinking; to pay attention to the winds of change; to negotiate so everyone wins; to identify your own biases; and to prioritize self-care.

In my mind, it is impossible to separate business development from human development. Our main assets are not our technical knowledge, abilities, or contacts but our energy, so I invite you to look at yourself and your business through the lens of my failures and learnings. To notice how ephemeral our passage through the world is and freely decide to create and amplify value.

Are you ready to begin?

CHAPTER 1

INVEST IN YOUR CORE AREA

When Juan, my college roommate's brother-in-law, approached me during the cocktail party to talk about a seventy-five-acre parcel on the shores of the Río Claro, it seemed like a good investment. Between 1994 and 2000, an aquaculture company called SAGRO had operated on that land, leveraging nearly seventy fishponds to produce tilapia—until ELN (National Liberation Army) guerrillas entered the company's plant, kidnapped two technicians, and detonated explosives. Unable to produce fish, SAGRO was liquidated, and the area was abandoned. Now the ponds were giant flower pots for plants, shrubs, and trees, but the infrastructure on which to base an aquaculture business remained in place.

Juan, who had been a partner at the growing company, said the price and opportunity were good. Since the public safety situation had improved, we could either take advantage of the existing infrastructure or let the land appreciate before selling it. Both scenarios sounded favorable to me, so without further consideration, I agreed to buy the land with Juan and my old roommate.

At the time, I was thirty-four and the executive vice president of Premex, but I was interested in making investments outside the family business. Like many people, I had always thought tilapia was the protein of the future, that it was a more efficient and economical alternative to chicken, beef, or pork since it requires fewer resources to produce. So when my mentor, Enrique, the president of one of Premex's main customers, wanted to get in on starting a new fish farm, it seemed like a good investment. We proposed the idea to a number of well-known and respected entrepreneurs in the region—including my father—who all enthusiastically joined us.

The ten of us who started El Rosario had a clear intent: to restore SAGRO's infrastructure and become the largest exporter of farmed tilapia in Colombia. On top of that, we agreed to generate formal employment in the area since it had been severely affected by violence and illegality. With the collective experience of all ten partners, it was hard not to believe that we would succeed.

Yet one of the striking facts about El Rosario is that no one but Juan had any real experience in aquaculture. So when he left, which I will discuss more in Chapter 2, the remaining nine of us each had a significant investment in the company but no specific knowledge to guide our growth. That meant we depended on administrators and third parties to define strategy—and that our learning curve was unusually steep.

Nobody should be a leading investor in a business that is not in his or her core area, his or her center of experience. Five years have now passed since the liquidation of El Rosario, and that is one of the lessons most present in my mind. It sounds obvious, but the risk of ending up where I did is high. Without realizing what you are doing, it is possible to join a business as a passive investor and end up carrying it on your back to try to save it.

EVALUATING PROPOSALS

Now, it is easy to recognize in hindsight that I should have more carefully evaluated the proposal to set up a fish farm, but my ego led me to believe that I knew about aquaculture because it was covered in some college classes I took and because it is a topic I have followed over the years. I know, for instance, that aquatic protein is very efficient and therefore important for the future of world nutrition. (Producing a kilogram of chicken requires 1.3 to 1.6 kilograms of balanced feed, while a kilo of pork requires 3.0 to 3.2 kilograms of balanced feed.[1] A kilo of tilapia, on the other hand, requires 1.5 to 2.5 in pond environments and 1.0 to 1.71 in cage environments.[2]) Peter Drucker, the most important management professor and author of the twentieth century, said that aquaculture, not the internet, was going to be the business of the twenty-first.[3]

But it is one thing to have data and theory, and it is another to have experience. Experience comes only from doing something again and again, from spending thousands of hours circling a question, adjusting variables, and applying lessons learned. Neither I nor the other partners had this. We could invest all the money we wanted, but we did not have the experience needed to transform that investment into wealth.

When all is said and done, the value that amplifies capital lies within us. We should apply a huge discount rate to industries we are unfamiliar with.

1   Pradeep, "The Ultimate Guide to FCR (Feed Conversion Ratio)," *NavFarm* (blog), September 22, 2020, https://www.navfarm.com/blog/fcr-guide/.

2   Samuel Bekele Mengistu et al., "A Systematic Literature Review of the Major Factors Causing Yield Gap by Affecting Growth, Feed Conversion Ratio and Survival in Nile Tilapia (*Oreochromis niloticus*)," *Reviews in Aquaculture* 12, no. 2 (May 2020): 525, https://doi.org/10.1111/raq.12331.

3   James Wright, "Offshore Opportunity," SeafoodSource, September 6, 2012, https://www.seafoodsource.com/news/aquaculture/offshore-opportunity.

Imagine a group of entrepreneurs showed up at my office and said, "Alejandro, guess what? We want to invite you to partner with us in a company that will produce micro-ingredients for functional foods." In a meeting like that, I would sit there and bombard them with questions: What scientific evidence supports their plan? What chemical processes are they experimenting with? How are they going to resolve X-problem?

I would have dozens and dozens of questions because I have lived that business. I know it well. Maybe I would conclude the meeting by saying they have a promising project but it involves this risk, that risk, and the other risk. Because I understand the challenges involved, I would apply a very high discount rate.

In the finance sector, "discount rate" typically refers to the interest rate used to determine the present value of future cash flows. It is a key concept in financial calculations and decision-making processes, serving several important functions:

- It accounts for the time value of money, recognizing that a dollar today is worth more than a dollar in the future due to its potential earning capacity.
- It adjusts for risk, with higher discount rates applied to more uncertain future cash flows.
- It helps in comparing investments with different time-frames and risk profiles.

The problem is, entrepreneurs tend to quote low discount rates for areas we do not know as well as our own.

Let's say someone else showed up at my office the next day and said, "Alejandro, I want to invite you to join a business. We are going to set up a columbite-tantalite distribution firm in China. We already have suppliers in Brazil, ready to participate.

Look at this Excel sheet. The business is a gold mine. Every cell phone contains this mineral. It is the business of the future. Let's get going as distributors, and we will reap tremendous returns." In that case, I would not have so many questions.

I know that, in general terms, the potential of the mineral nicknamed coltan appears unlimited and that Chinese industries need more and more of it. If I had confidence in the person who brought me the proposal, if that person knew how to present the idea, and if I had enough capital and uncontrolled ambition, I would assign a discount rate much lower than the one for the business I know. I would imagine greater profitability because I do not know all the variables that could depress the profits, but that imagined profitability would significantly increase the probability that I would make a mistake. (Full disclosure: because of a personal decision, I do not invest in mining or mine products.)

It is very different when you encounter a complication while you are leading a business you know well. At Iluma Alliance, the ecosystem of companies (including Premex) that I currently lead, we have risked the future of the company at least four times. Suddenly, we reach a crossroads where any decision we make is almost an existential one. Luckily, the experience, talent, and commitment of the nearly one thousand people who work there has allowed us to keep the company going while we learn what we need to re-adapt ourselves to our environment.

We tend to overvalue what we know less about and to undervalue what we know well. That is why it is important to identify and utilize what makes you unique.

I am not implying that because you are an engineer, your business has to keep away from anything that has to do with the humanities. Or because you are an agronomist, you have to avoid active investment in the IT sector. Not at all. Hybrid talents, such strange birds, are needed now more than ever. They grow out of deep curiosity, which the world needs so much.

I am always inspired by people who do something exceptionally well and want to complement that with a field of knowledge they so far lack. That is how new paths are opened, new competencies are developed, and more value is created. However, you will get farther if you take advantage of your innate strengths.

Dan Sullivan, co-founder of Strategic Coach®, has a program called Unique Ability®. It consists of identifying the characteristics, values, and abilities unique to each individual, the things the individual loves to do and, furthermore, does extremely well. The underlying idea is that if you are clear about your Unique Ability, you will connect in a better way with your goal and be able to devote yourself to your particular calling.

My ability has to do with using curiosity to see the world as full of possibilities. This allows me to simplify problems and communicate them in a way that catalyzes action. Nothing interests me more than contributing to the construction of a better world, a world nourished in all its dimensions.

I did not find this clarity of purpose until recently. Perhaps if I had had it when the fish farm was first proposed to me, I could have better evaluated the opportunity.

A fish farm depends on efficiency. To become profitable, it demands administration and millimetric controls, so as to produce maximum units of quality output—fish—at limited cost per unit. It is not a business offering room for imagining and designing products or services (e.g., digital services or media) that can be sold multiple times once they are produced.

None of the required abilities for aquaculture—monitoring tasks, controlling processes, optimizing production—are part of my unique skillset. I can do those things, but they do not come from my core. They wear me out rather than motivating me to create value. Efficiency in production systems is a necessary and valuable talent that many people have. But not me.

The core of the organization in which I now invest my heart and soul is animal and human nutrition, micronutrition, and functional nutrition. El Rosario taught me that to depart from this core is dangerous; doing so deprives me of the energy I need to create priorities and strategies for Iluma, an organization selected by the market for its nourishing products. Anything related to my unique ability is an opportunity; anything else is a diversion.

Identifying our unique abilities is useful in filtering the invitations we might receive and the opportunities we might see. Today, the aquaculture venture would not make it through my filter—at least, not as a primary investment. I might, however, use it as a learning opportunity.

INVESTING IN LEARNING

I am a passive investor in several companies. I invest in shares of companies that I like and in endeavors that inspire and stimulate my imagination. But to be an investor-leader—that is, to serve on the board and guide the business, to make recommendations to the team, to identify opportunities and threats—I have not done that since El Rosario.

With El Rosario, I learned that eventually I will run into difficulties specific to whatever business I invest in. And it will likely take me longer to learn how to solve those problems than it will take the company to fail. That is an unjustified waste of professional energy. (I suspect that waste of energy is what sowed the seeds of the depression I fell into shortly after El Rosario.)

Since El Rosario closed, I have avoided investing in businesses over which I do not have control or, at least, influence. If I am going to be a passive associate at a high level of investment, then I need, at a minimum, a channel of communication with members of the board so I know how things are going and can intervene as needed. Since that is not my usual practice, normally I invest for education or for pleasure.

Sometimes I invest in the stock of companies that are not within my core area, but I do so as an educational rather than an investment activity. When I see, for example, a company taking a new track in the biotechnology area, I decide to buy a share. Why? Because I think, *That is the way the world is trending.* Plus, with that investment, I can get important reports and news, as well as feel part of the company's evolution. It is a passive investment, yet I am learning.

One thing I wished I had learned sooner? How to optimize group dynamics.

CHAPTER 2

OPTIMIZE GROUP DYNAMICS

During El Rosario's first stockholder meeting, we decided that Juan would be our managing director. After all, he had been a partner at SAGRO and had the right disposition, contacts, and free time to handle the role. Then my partners made an additional decision that took me by surprise: I, the youngest and least expert, would be the chairman of the board. They wanted to give me the opportunity to learn by doing.

Having run a very successful chicken company, Juan started managing El Rosario as if there were no limits to its capital. He would present us business plans that looked wonderful and contracts that had been signed by two or three partners, and the rest of us would sign off without much thought. We were so confident in him that we gave him almost complete autonomy from the board.

Getting the fish cultivation process underway cost much more than we expected, so we put in more capital. We bought a million tilapia. We hired 110 people from the region, most of whom had been directly affected by violence. We wanted to do well not only to recoup and multiply our investment, but also to create value in an area that had suffered so much and lacked nearby state or private companies.

In addition, each partner signed an individual commitment to pay. That is, if the company defaulted on the collective debt, the bank could come and collect the entire amount from any one of us. We were steeped in the euphoria of creating something new, and nobody wanted to rain on the parade.

But then everything started to go wrong. Our tilapia grew so large that workers started calling them *tiburones* (sharks). A tree that contained a toxin deadly to tilapia fell in the river, killing thousands of fish every morning. Finally, we found and negotiated a deal with a distributor who was open to buying our whole output, but Juan threatened to resign because they were Ecuadorian.

Our managing director never formally resigned his post; he just picked up his briefcase, stood up from the boardroom table, and left. In the resulting confusion, everybody looked to me as chairman of the board, saying that we needed to find another director. So, two years after we had launched El Rosario, I became responsible for figuring out how we had gotten into a debt deeper than any of our ponds—and how we could get out of it.

In retrospect, I agreed to chair the board because I desired external validation. Pride in my title kept me from taking a hard look at our decision-making process and seeing that we were prioritizing cohesion above all.

PRIORITIZING COHESION

In 1974, business administration expert Jerry Harvey described a visit to his in-laws' home in the journal *Organizational Dynam-*

ics.[4] It was 104 degrees, and a dust storm had coated everything in maddening, fine-grained topsoil, but the family was having a good time playing dominoes on the porch. Then Harvey's father-in-law suggested that they make the fifty-three-mile trek to Abilene for lunch.

Four hours later, when the family returned to the house exhausted, Harvey's mother-in-law admitted that she had not enjoyed the trip. One by one, each person said that they would have rather stayed home, but they did not want to ruin everyone else's fun. Even Harvey's father-in-law said he only suggested the trip to be sociable.

Harvey could not believe it. How could a group of sensible adults decide to go, of their own volition, to a place none of them actually wanted to go?

The Abilene paradox, a form of groupthink in which the group makes a decision against the interests of all its members, is one of the most useful lenses through which to examine what happened with El Rosario. The minor difference is that Harvey's family trip lasted one afternoon, while our business venture lasted over a decade. Still, in the end, we ran into the same confusion: how did we get stuck on this journey?

CONFLICTS OF INTEREST

It is true that the decision to create the fish farm was an enthusiastic one, representing the individual desire of each of the partners. No one felt obligated, nobody accepted just to avoid problems with the others. But the Abilene paradox began to emerge soon after we started the company. I was not conscious

---

4   Jerry B. Harvey, "The Abilene Paradox: The Management of Agreement," *Organizational Dynamics* 3, no. 1 (Summer 1974): 63–80, https://doi.org/10.1016/0090-2616(74)90005-9.

of this at the moment, but in retrospect I can see that the conditions for expressing individual preferences within the group of investors—the conditions for raising one's hand to disagree—were terrible. There were too many conflicts of interest. When the company was finally liquidated, I carried out a simple, productive exercise. I took a blank sheet of paper and drew a diagram of the stakeholders (in this case, all the members of the board). Then I started drawing connecting lines, each one representing a relationship outside the aquaculture company (e.g., commercial relationships, familial ties, friendships). Within a few minutes, I had detected several faults in this system.

Among the ten partners, there were two sets of brothers, three sets of in-laws, a father and son, and a boss and his subordinate. What's more, the head of one of Premex's main client companies was there. In those circumstances, all of us were watching our backs. I was not going to contradict a leading customer, so as not to injure Premex; the brothers wanted to minimize friction between themselves; the in-laws privileged that relationship over the needs of the aquaculture firm; and so on.

Without realizing it, we created a fundamentally inhibited group. We were all inclined to celebrate the company's success, but we would not risk having difficult conversations or surfacing productive tensions. And that aversion to controversy cut off, right at the roots, any possibility of collective creation, of exploring the unknown (with all its difficulties and compensations).

A board in which dissent and healthy friction are impossible will say yes to everything. It will pour in money. It will give a green light to taking on debt. And if anything goes wrong, its members will justify themselves by saying that they never really agreed, but everyone else was so united that they chose to go with the flow. Simple.

HOMOGENOUS GROUPS

Besides everyone having conflicting interests, the El Rosario board was too homogeneous. We started with an obvious handicap: all the partners were men. We were also all entrepreneurs native to Antioquia who were focused on agribusiness. That lack of diversity significantly reduced the company's possibilities. Beginning the business venture with brute force, for instance, exemplifies unrestricted masculinity. We wanted to impose our interests on the needs of others—mainly, on those of nature and of the market. Also, each of us growing up in a culture that teaches men to hide our vulnerability led to no one daring to appear insecure in front of the others. Express train to Abilene!

In the 1970s, when he coined the term "groupthink," psychologist Irving Janis described some symptoms that manifest in groups affected by this phenomenon. For example, the illusion of invulnerability—"We are ten successful men with the capital to make the fish-farming venture profitable, so what can go wrong?" An unquestionable belief in the morality of the group—"Setting up an industrial operation on the Río Claro has no negative impact on this ecosystem or the communities downstream." The presence of "guard dogs" that act as a barrier against any divergent point of view. And the stigmatization of anyone who challenges the group. Janis also mentions self-censorship and the illusion of unanimity as signs that the group is not making comprehensive judgments about realities.[5]

As if our homogeneity was not enough, the board did not have formal rules for decision-making because our leadership

---

5   Irving L. Janis, *Victims of Groupthink: A Psychological Study of Foreign-Policy Decisions and Fiascoes* (Houghton Mifflin Company, 1972), 36–43.

was confused. In other words, the role each member fulfilled conflicted with the title they held.

IDENTIFYING EVERYONE'S ROLE

Even though I was named chairman of the board, the managing director, Juan, and my mentor, Enrique, had the most prominent voices in board meetings. They were the ones leading our conversations. Sometimes it felt like I was the so-called leader to divert attention from their decisions; other times it felt like I was the face of the company because I was a "good boy."

Every person in a group inevitably fulfills a role beyond their formal title (e.g., designer, manager, operative). Think about your closest associates: There are people who tend to cut through tensions with their sense of humor, others who are inveterate skeptics. There are those who help connect the dots between what others say, those who tend to raise extreme ideas or uncomfortable topics, those who invite contributions from people who have stayed quiet, etc. The group assigns these roles unconsciously. They are systematic forces over which no one has any initial control. The group places each person in the space where he or she fits best—whether to move the group in the direction of its goal or to sabotage it.

So, I was chairman of the board in name, but I had neither the experience nor the authority to make or suggest alternative operational decisions. This was in part because I worried too much about my fellow board members' impression of me. I was the youngest, and I felt pressure to demonstrate exceptional skill to these other businessmen whom I admired. That constant feeling of being judged robbed me of spontaneity and made me more vulnerable to placing the group's view over my own intuition.

In the end, the board was right about me: as a good boy, I

wanted to minimize the blow to our finances and our reputations. Consciously or not, most partners distanced themselves, assuming I would take on El Rosario's burdens. And I did because I have an inflated sense of duty and also because of the individual debt commitments I previously described. I feared that the bank would come to extract our collective debt from me or from my father.

It is very hard to identify the role one is playing within a system. Most times our role is the result of unconscious behaviors, and we do not have the necessary distance to define them. However, one of the lessons I have learned is that it does not really matter who is the leader as long as they have the chutzpah required for the role.

CHUTZPAH

A Yiddish concept, *chutzpah* refers to the courage to raise one's voice, to say what one thinks without worrying about the judgments of others. It honors freedom of expression.

In El Rosario's board meetings, I did not display this trait. Even though I did not want the company to start on such a large scale, even though I would have preferred not to sign the individual commitment to pay the debt, and even though many management decisions seemed inappropriate to me, I prioritized group stability over my own chutzpah.

Now I am much more aware of the risks of self-censorship. I do not mean that in every meeting I act in opposition or I impose my own interpretations. But if I am not feeling confident about expressing myself, that sets off an alarm. Most likely, I am not the only one feeling that way; there are probably unconscious currents pushing the group someplace it may not want to go.

If I could have a chat with the thirty-four-year-old Alejandro who was appointed "chairman of the board," I would advise him to have the courage—the chutzpah—to propose that the board adopt a different method of making decisions, such as facilitating conversations. Such a method might be slower, provoke more friction, and feel more uncomfortable, but it would be more respectful of the talents of the investors.

If a business venture looks simple, if people claim it needs only investment funds and an administrator, the best thing to do is cover your ears and not let yourself be seduced. Value is created among people who listen to each other, who are not afraid to question their ways of thinking—because they are confident that the goal, which should be the north star of the venture, will unify and orient them.

CONVERSATIONS

I am sure that the story of El Rosario would have ended very differently if, among the ten partners, we had possessed the humility and courage to have some difficult conversations. Despite our homogeneity, we had a lot of group experience and knowledge. But those assets were not applied to our purpose because we did not know how to listen to each other, or we did not want to do so.

A better company would facilitate its members' exploration of their abilities, but the only way to do that is through dialogue. Conversation is a creative act. It is where value begins to be created, so as to be offered to the world later on.

Since the aquaculture experience, I have felt that stimulating conversation is a priority. That is a huge challenge, especially in Latin America, due perhaps to our colonial past, our coming from several generations obliged to believe dogmatically in institutions and authority. But a company accrues competitive advantage if it can create the conditions for everyone—regardless of position—to feel backing and support for expressing themselves, including questioning organizational policies or orders from above.

At Iluma, we have prioritized conversation by creating an internal communication campaign called "A Safe Zone for Controversy." Through horizontal conversation, we are able to generate new knowledge, challenge established practices, and avoid groupthink.

AVOIDING GROUPTHINK

Over the past five decades, there have been countless articles about how to prevent groupthink. One practical strategy is to analyze whether a group's decisions challenge the status quo or whether they conform to what has worked in the past. A system constricted by groupthink tends to follow established practices because if they fail to function now, it is easy to evade responsibility. Therefore, it is important to discuss whether and how past solutions may be inappropriate for today's challenges.

With El Rosario, for example, we never discussed whether it was really a good idea to restore SAGRO's infrastructure and build another fish farm. We were ten people with the goal of making a profitable investment, yet no one asked whether there was any downside to mounting such an operation on that tract of land. What if the previous fish farm was never successful because of its location and the attendant costs associated with being so far from Medellín or Bogotá? No one asked that. No one questioned if SAGRO's initial decision to locate an aquaculture plant in that location was a mistake.

There are other useful recommendations for avoiding

groupthink, such as assigning one or two participants in any decision-making space a formal role as dissenters (also known as devil's advocates). Devil's advocates have the group's explicit authorization to challenge any emerging consensus so as to make the discussion more complex. Another possible solution is to have individuals write down their opinions on a subject before it is discussed. That way, the group can recover its diversity of perspectives and can challenge a false consensus.

Not everything that happened with El Rosario can be explained through the lens of groupthink, however. Another factor is that we saw business as a numbers game rather than a biological system.

CHAPTER 3

RECOGNIZE COMPANIES AS BIOLOGICAL SYSTEMS

When the board tasked the managing director with restoring the existing aquaculture infrastructure on our land, he presented a business plan that explained how we would reorganize the facility and finance the venture. The Excel sheets looked promising, so we signed without much conversation.

Once the ponds were repaired and the processing plant was ready, Juan set up a factory to make polystyrene shipping boxes on-site, saying that would be better than sending them from Medellín. He then arranged to buy other equipment whose purpose was not really clear to us. And that is not even counting the tilapia we bought and workers we hired, which I mentioned in Chapter 1.

Within months, each partner's investment had grown exponentially. It seemed like we were throwing all our chips into the pot with every new attempt, every adjustment, requiring still more. That is a dangerous situation because in such circumstances—maybe as a protective mechanism—the ego takes over the controls, and the mind does not want to learn.

By the time we were halfway down the road, it was clear that this way of beginning had been a mistake, that our behavior was affected by a slew of "traps" we had set for ourselves. In the most stressful moments, in nights of insomnia, I remembered the first spreadsheet presentations, when the numbers looked perfect. I have always been good at math, and in truth, it was a promising operation. On paper. Only at the end, in trying to understand why things always go bad when we start off too big, did I connect the dots and understand something that radically changed my way of looking at business.

The problem was not the numbers. Or, better put, the problem was trusting exclusively in the numbers. All my life, I had believed that companies operated mainly according to the dictates of economics and finance—until I reread Darwin and changed the paradigm.

Companies are not abstractions, not mathematical models that can assure success if they are well formulated. No. As I heard the consultant Alejandro Salazar say in 2005, companies are complex biological systems. They operate more according to evolutionary dynamics than abstractions.

APPLYING EVOLUTIONARY THEORY TO BUSINESS

"Nothing in biology makes sense except in the light of evolution," wrote the Russian-American geneticist Theodosius Dobzhansky in 1973.[6] The theory put forward by Darwin remains robust in spite of 150 years of experiments and permanent scrutiny.

---

6   Theodosius Dobzhansky, "Nothing in Biology Makes Sense Except in the Light of Evolution," *The American Biology Teacher* 35, no. 3 (March 1973): 125, https://doi.org/10.2307/4444260.

For my purpose in this chapter—to show the close relationship between businesses and biology—the vocabulary of evolution is indispensable.

No biological system evolves on a large scale. Variations or differentiations always occur on a small scale within a population, and the mutations most favored in the competition for resources are the ones "naturally selected" and passed on to future generations. The theory of natural selection can be summed up in three verbs: differentiate, select, and amplify. Darwin 101. The same is true for business.

We have always been told that companies respond to supply and demand. I do not believe that. Business is pure biology.

Enterprises create value. For whom? For their customers. The market is the ecosystem within which we relate, and within the ecosystem, there are two requisites for success. One is to conserve the ability to create value; the other is to capture a piece of this value for future uses. Those uses include amplifying the business, guaranteeing returns to investors, and providing collateral benefits to stakeholders.

The key thing to recognize is that when it comes to businesses, entrepreneurs have power over only two of the three evolutionary stages: differentiation and amplification. Selection is out of our control, as the competition takes place exclusively in the market and in the hands of potential customers.

I will discuss each of these three stages in turn.

DIFFERENTIATION

After graduating from Zamorano as an agronomist, I went to the University of Florida in Gainesville for another bachelor's degree, this time in agribusiness. In 1997, I returned to Colombia wanting to take on a business project outside of the family firm. I didn't want to be seen as "daddy's boy" who found himself "running" a company without effort or merit.

However, my father was as straightforward as he was practical. "Alejo," he asked me, "why do you want to retrace the whole family history when you can, instead, keep building on what we are now?" That reassured me. The emphasis on "keeping building" meant that my place in the company would depend on the effort I actually put in.

I joined Premex as a marketing assistant, spending hours in a corner of the factory analyzing data and writing reports for the relevant subdirectors. One day, my father asked me to go with him on a visit to a small company he had just bought. It was what we called, in Colombia, a *tarroquímica*, a small factory that made additives and sold them wholesale in big, plastic containers. He bought it for a strategic reason: as a parallel business owned by one of Premex's executives, it was generating a problematic conflict of interest.

The factory was in Sabaneta, at that time a newly industrializing rural area a half hour from Medellín. We met the four collaborators—Libardo, Ómar, Óscar, and Melquisedec—and toured the plant in five minutes. When we left, my father pulled a set of keys out of his pocket and handed them to me. "You are the manager of this company. Let us know when we can help you."

Adiquim became my school and my laboratory, literally and metaphorically. I started using information I found using Altavista (this was shortly before Google) to learn more about chemical processes and creating additives. I then found a reference point, a model: Anitox, located in the United States.

After I studied all the available information, we began mixing in our factory to see what might emerge from our chemical reactions. "This purple color? That means we did it!" We celebrated as if we had discovered the philosopher's stone.

It was a kind of work inspired by enjoyment, curiosity, and learning by doing. All on a small scale.

I did not have children yet, so I spent hours and hours at the plant. I remember one time staying there until three in the morning with Melquisedec, dozens of tools scattered on the floor as we tried to fix the mixing machine. I was not a chemist, but I had some foundational knowledge from my study at Zamorano, and I loved being in an environment where doubts and puzzles were just a world waiting to be explored, a world that once in a while rewarded us with discoveries.

One of our challenges was producing organic minerals. Nobody was doing that in Colombia, and the process was a mystery. After much trial and error, we succeeded in making them with the rudimentary equipment we had, and that changed everything. The first year, Adiquim grew five-fold from its original size. Four years later, we had a big factory and were exporting to other countries.

Being a Colombian company that could make organic products and offer them much more cheaply differentiated us in the market of feed distributors. Later, I learned that value is created in the intersection between what makes a company different and what makes it relevant. But there is a cardinal rule: what differentiates you today will eventually become the industry standard. To maintain your position, you have to keep updating and redefining what makes you unique.

Unlike what happened a decade later with the fish farm, everything started off small with Adiquim. We grew naturally, not forcing anything, and no one came to inundate us with capital. Everything was done with self-generated resources. In turn, the market selected us.

SELECTION

El Rosario grew by leaps and bounds without us waiting for a single customer to choose us. We assumed that a good product was enough to make buyers appear, which was the root of our disadvantage in negotiating with distributors. They knew that we were desperate to make sales and that they had more room to maneuver than we did.

Eventually, we sold tons and tons of tilapia, but by then, we were so bogged down with debt that we never managed to pay it off, no matter how hard we tried. Selection occurred but at the wrong time: when we were already a big company, compromised by our initial bad decisions.

Selection is the evolutionary stage over which entrepreneurs have no control; it is in the hands of the customers, the market. You can offer diamonds at the price of eggs, but if your market does not find diamonds valuable, it will go for eggs instead. Businesses are complex systems, and their success depends on many unknown variables. You may adjust one variable, but since it is linked to many more, you may be changing something else that, at first glance, seems completely unrelated.

Selection can be a great source of humility. Believing things will go well because you have got great ideas is an illusion, even a kind of arrogance. Genius does not exist outside of a system. "Ideas are a dime a dozen," as the Silicon Valley saying has it.

I believe that selection arises, in principle, from a genuine desire for cooperation. Entrepreneurs' priorities should not be to enrich themselves but to offer the world opportunities to enrich itself. This can take many forms: services, products, processes, solutions. But whatever you offer the market, you should have a very clear intent to improve people's lives. If a business foregrounds its own benefit, the system will take charge of neutralizing it; if the project of generating value is focused on the customer, the business is more likely to flourish.

Let's start, then, from this notion of a will to cooperate and posit that the value being offered is a distinctive one. Is that a guarantee of being chosen? Unfortunately, no. Because you do not get to define the value you create.

Under free conditions, value stems from market competition, from the customer. The probability of being selected grows if what is being offered gives customers more opportunities than they had before. It is not a zero-sum transaction. Both parties are creating more possibilities and, thus, the whole system improves.

Asimetrix™, one of the companies in the Iluma ecosystem, designs intelligent solutions for producers of animal protein. The hypothesis is that producers can optimize their care of their animals if they take full advantage of the data provided within the corral. So, we have patented a technology called the "Internet of Animals"® that gathers and processes real-time data, enabling customers to monitor the well-being and productive activity of their animals.

We started in some experimental farms, and now Asimetrix has the ability to measure the health of a herd by the animals' movements, feeding times, temperature, or eating patterns. All this information—previously held only in the minds of the animals' caretakers—becomes a useful tool for identifying important signals. If the animals make or stop making a certain sound, the system can call attention to it and warn about the risk of illness because the system has already learned from similar signals in the past. Thus, the producer can react on time and avoid the animals' illness getting worse.

That sounds great, but we still cannot step into the market and require anyone to choose us. It is thanks to various cycles of modification and to joint work with producers that Asimetrix solutions have now been chosen by important actors in the market.

Selection occurs on a daily basis, a form of democratic voting in which the polls are always open. The moment our solutions stop creating value, buyers will stop choosing us. The same thing is true if a new and different solution on the market allows the customer to better adapt to current challenges.

Sometimes the leaders of Iluma come to me with problems, saying, "Alejo, we are going to have trouble if we do this or stop doing that." My response is always the same: "If we have trouble, that is because it is what we deserve. If we are not good enough to deserve to exist, that is a problem of our making. It is no one else's fault: you cannot force anyone to choose us."

AMPLIFICATION

Before becoming what it is today, Asimetrix was, for quite a while, a money sink. Since the company was my personal project, the team there assumed we had unlimited resources, that they just needed to come in to the office and present me with a few attractive opportunities in order to walk out with a blank check. And that is how things went for some years—until we realized that instead of creating value, we were destroying it.

Since the team had abundant resources, we ended up pursuing dozens of projects that had not been chosen by our customers. As with the fish farm, we did not wait to validate hypotheses. We wanted to take giant steps right away. But as Eduardo Salazar, a strategy consultant and friend, said, "You do not grow in order to be profitable. If you are profitable, you grow."

The scarcest resource in the world of opportunities is focus, and focus is achieved through restrictions. When establishing your business, first:

- Build long-term, mutually beneficial relationships with customers and stakeholders, as well as prioritize activities and initiatives that generate the most value for them.
- Invest time and resources in areas where the company has unique expertise and competitive advantage.
- Build a shared set of values and practices that align with the company's goals and that foster employee engagement.
- Cultivate a can-do attitude and growth mindset throughout the company, empowering individuals to utilize their unique abilities, experiment, and learn from failure.
- Break down silos to allow for the free flow of ideas and resources across the organization.
- Create mechanisms for gathering and acting on feedback from employees, customers, and partners.

Then, to amplify your business:

- Update and expand the company's knowledge base through research, training, and learning initiatives.
- Integrate cutting-edge technologies to improve processes, products, and services.
- Regularly review and adjust how resources are distributed to ensure they are supporting key growth initiatives.
- Stay flexible, ready to pivot in response to market changes and new opportunities.

Again, restriction at the beginning is fundamental. A good jockey knows how to save a horse's strength for the proper moment. You should not fall to the rear of the pack by reducing your chances to get ahead, but neither should you give free rein to your horse. You do not want to start so far ahead that your horse wears out before reaching the finish line.

It is pure regulation of energy. You have to restrict and stay in the pack. Only on the last lap, when your horse has proven its ability to meet the prevailing average, do you give free rein and use that surprise store of energy to win.

TAKING THOUGHTFUL ACTION

If I were to have another fish farm, I would not start with seventy ponds, a million animals, and such a big installation. I would start with ten pools, learning to understand the natural processes, identifying variables, and experimenting until I found what would make us stand out. Then, at that scale, we would go to the market.

Would we surprise ourselves by shaking up the industry? If so, if the market began to ask for more, we would gradually ramp up production. If not, if the market ignored us and did not recognize the value that we thought we were offering, we would fall back, make adjustments—which, thanks to the size of the experiment, would not cost us that much—and try again with a new version.

The downside—that maybe the business would never take off—would be minimal because we would have only put up enough capital to learn. But the upside—that the market selected us and amplified our production—would be very big. That would have been the ideal scenario, but as my Aunt Inés used to say, "The universe rewards action, not thought."

Still, you do not want to act just because—throwing more and more resources at problems is not always the solution, as you will see in Chapter 4. Instead, it is important to cultivate a growth mindset so that you can take thoughtful action.

CULTIVATE A GROWTH MINDSET

Between 2011 and 2017, El Rosario began exporting millions of dollars' worth of fresh tilapia a year. The board held meetings that brought out the best in us, that rekindled our initial enthusiasm. But the money that finally came in was not enough to repay our debt, and new problems arose at every turn.

One day, we received a call that the river had flooded and carried off some tilapia. When we went to the plant to calculate the damage, we realized that "some" was a euphemism. The storm had carried off nearly all the fish.

Luckily, we had insurance to cover such eventualities, but when the insurance firm paid us for the damage, they also told us they would not renew the policy. They did not want to assume the high risk of another flood. So, we had to take on even more debt to fence in all the ponds—each one half the size of a soccer field—in order to keep any future river surges from carrying the tilapia away. It made for a strange scene: a valley with seventy artificial ponds, each caged like an enormous cell, as if the place were a jail for water.

Our second managing director redesigned many of our

processes, as well as gave us better insight into some of the company's unnecessary investments. He converted one of our warehouses, for instance, into a repository of expensive and useless machinery. He also created nutritional, cultural, and commercial programs intended to link the nearby communities to the progress of the company. But after a winter full of deluges that cost us most of our inventory, an El Niño that dried up the streams and dramatically increased the cost of all our inputs, and the value of the dollar plummeting, he left. He did not feel comfortable putting so much effort into a business that produced only mediocre returns.

The third managing director of El Rosario negotiated a "currency forward" deal with the bank to reduce the company's risk when the exchange rate fluctuated. So, if the bank lent us a dollar, and the value of that currency fell, we would not have to pay back as much. It seemed like a good decision at the time, but as soon as we signed that agreement, the value of the dollar began to climb. In theory, a strong dollar meant more income from international sales, but then the international price of tilapia began to fall. As our debt grew and our revenue dropped, the pressure became too much for the third director. He left too.

When we hired El Rosario's fourth and last managing director, we decided to seek out new investment partners. We had already put in more money than each of us could really afford, but we felt we needed new capital to restructure the company for one last attempt. We assembled a very good pitch that recognized the difficulties but also the potential of the fish farm. We pointed to the areas where an injection of capital would bring an almost certain return.

Soon, we found two investment funds interested in joining us and began working out the formal details with one of them. That meant ten months of preparing documentation, creating conditions, resolving legal details, etc. Finally, when everything was ready to sign, a change of leadership at the fund undermined the agreement, which collapsed. We were alone, in debt, and without the energy to try to find new partners all over again.

With each new problem, we became more and more anxious. We knew that El Rosario was not going to recover as long as its board members were 150 kilometers away in Medellín, trying to run a business over the telephone. As long as each of us had primary commitments to other firms.

For example, I had recently become the president of Premex and was looking to expand internationally—a decision that led to the birth of Iluma Alliance. But I knew as soon as El Rosario stopped making payments on the debt, the bank would collect from whichever partner it chose (the Russian roulette of the individual debt arrangement), and it would surely go after whoever had the most liquidity. The probability of this being my father and me was high. As a result, I felt even more pressure to keep on seeking solutions to a problem that seemed insoluble.

Over time, I have realized that the creation of value depends less on the talent and ability of an individual and his or her team and more on the mindset from which they operate. You can have all the necessary forms of competence to be successful in the market, but that is no guarantee that you will generate value. Because, in the end, wealth depends above all on the mentality of the entrepreneur. Abilities are an advantage, of course, but mindset is the lever that makes the difference. The fish farm provides a clear example: collectively, we had sufficient capacities, resources, and experience to set up a profitable business, but we did not realize we were trapped in a kind of mentality that sabotaged our growth.

IDENTIFYING YOUR CURRENT MINDSET

Often we are conscious of *what* we think, but less conscious of *why*. We do not realize that our mindset is the lens through which we make sense of our experiences, that the beliefs we hold shape our thoughts and actions. Furthermore, according to Stanford professor Carol Dweck, author of the 2006 book *Mindset: The New Psychology of Success*, there are two kinds of mindsets: "fixed" and "growth."[7] So, let me share a brief anecdote that effectively illustrates both.

During the 1989 International Cup in Japan, soccer star Leonel Álvarez was asked, "How do you feel? Are you feeling at all afraid?" After all, his team, Atlético Nacional (the first Colombian team to become the champions of South America), was about to face AC Milan, an Italian team with much more experience in international tournaments. A team that already had an International Cup on its trophy shelf.

Álvarez, instinctively, turned the question around: "Afraid of what? It's eleven of us against eleven other guys and a ball."[8]

The reporter saw the game through the fixed-mindset lens, assuming that a Colombian team that was new to the global competition had to be inferior in ability to an established Italian team. Álvarez, on the other hand, saw the challenge from the growth mindset: the contest on the field would not involve history, or prestige, or the idea of Europe against South America. Álvarez saw it as one more game, so he was focused less on winning than on playing. (As it turned out, Nacional played a good game but lost at the last minute on a free-kick goal.)

---

7   Carol S. Dweck, *Mindset: The New Psychology of Success* (Ballantine Books, 2008), 6–7.

8   "Copa Intercontinental—Milán vs Atlético Nacional 1989," posted August 22, 2020, by Solo Fútbol, YouTube, 2 min., 11 sec., https://www.youtube.com/watch?v=SAOkO8ctyTA.

But how do you identify which mindset you currently operate from?

FIXED MINDSETS

Like many Latin Americans, I was brought up with a fixed mindset, more like the reporter than like Leonel. A fixed mindset is characterized by fear of our deficiencies being exposed, and typically, we compensate by having an exaggerated desire for control and external validation. As I have already described, this fixed mindset pushed me to accept the role of "chairman of the board" in the aquaculture company, even though I was obviously the one with the least experience.

A fixed mindset makes it hard to lead companies toward growth. Usually, if you bring that perspective to a position of authority within an organization, you will dictate more than ask questions; you will ignore criticism, delegate very little, and distrust a lot. People with fixed mindsets worry more about how they are viewed than about expanding their potentials and exploring opportunities. As Naval Ravikant puts it, they are more focused on the status game than the wealth game (with wealth understood, once again, as the capacity to create value).[9]

People who operate from a fixed mindset assume that, just as one is born with a certain body type or a certain skin color, traits such as intelligence, personality, and character are distinct and invariable. That is, one is born as a certain kind of person, and their traits cannot change. They think of intelligence as something that can be measured—with an IQ test, for instance—and they think that number defines us forever.

---

9   Eric Jorgenson, *The Almanack of Naval Ravikant: A Guide to Wealth and Happiness* (Magrathea Publishing, 2020), 73–74.

When confronting their failures, people with fixed mindsets withdraw and judge themselves harshly. To explain why they fell short of their goals, they resort to labels: "I am not good enough," "This is not for me," "I am an impostor." Often they become paralyzed and avoid exposing themselves to challenging circumstances, so as to avoid revealing their supposedly limited abilities.

GROWTH MINDSETS

People with growth mindsets come from a different place. They see themselves as malleable, adaptable, in a permanent process of change. Instead of seeing failure as a reason for shame, they take it as a learning experience. They welcome a crisis as an indicator of what they can change, a transition toward a state of greater self-knowledge. They think that, with effort and determination, they can develop new competencies and adapt themselves to meet challenges. They know that, to reach their potential, they have to persevere gracefully under adversity; that way, they find opportunities in both successes and defeats.

All of us act from both mindsets in different areas of our lives. Strengthening the growth mindset requires daily practice—requires "going to the gym," seeing every challenge as a chance to exercise adaptability.

Psychologically, the two mindsets are not mutually exclusive. One may have a growth mentality in business yet a fixed one in social or family relations, or vice versa. In general, I use mathematical thinking to solve problems and do not get frustrated if I do not find the solution right away. It is the complexity of business that attracts me, so I operate with a growth mindset.

When I joined the other investors to create El Rosario, however, I wanted to show I was "as good an entrepreneur" as they were. So, I got trapped in a fixed mindset. I prioritized status over cooperation, performance over enjoyment. I did not see the failure of the fish farm as something within the realm of possibility but something to be avoided at all costs so that I could protect my ego. Operating from that mindset, every obstacle generated stress and exhaustion.

WORKING THROUGH OBSTACLES

When I joined Harvard's Owner/President Management Program (OPM), a three-year program for owners or managing partners of companies, I realized that my colleagues, many of them executives and/or owners of billion-dollar corporations, did not have extra-terrestrial powers. They were ordinary people with one small distinguishing characteristic: their deep curiosity, which led to unexpected observations and value creation. They took pleasure in confronting obstacles, approaching business and learning from a growth mindset.

When we are operating from a fixed mindset, it seems impossible to think any other way. Fortunately, reality is different. The brain and body are flexible, and the patterns that have guided our actions—often against our own will—can change. Anyone can achieve a growth mindset.

STOICISM

One of the most striking characteristics of a person with a growth mindset is the ability to learn alongside adversity. That is also one of the principles of stoicism: Circumstances are unimportant. It doesn't matter whether what is happening is beneficial or adverse; what matters is meeting every moment with character and equanimity.

In his book *The Obstacle Is the Way*, Ryan Holiday says, "How about that business decision that turned out to be a mistake? Well, you had a hypothesis and it turned out to be wrong. Why should that upset you? It wouldn't piss off a scientist, it would help him. Maybe don't bet so much on it next time. And now you've learned two things: that your instinct was wrong, and the kind of appetite for risk you really have."[10]

Obstacles are part of the daily business experience. What's more, they are a natural part of the business environment. Even just having competitors in a market can create a pressure that can limit or inspire, depending on one's mindset.

The central premise of Holiday's book, based on the stoic outlook, is that there are no obstacles, just paths to explore. An enormous rock blocking the way might stop many people, making them interrupt their journeys. But for those with a growth mindset, the rock is not an obstacle but a sign that the road is different from how they thought it would be, so they need to search out other ways to go forward. That attitude is the path.

For stoics, life is permanent practice, and the most difficult experiences are opportunities to shed useless thoughts, strengthen character, and make proper decisions. There is no moment—happy or sad—from which one cannot learn. There is no moment that does not reaffirm the freedom and agency of those who live it.

In Latin, this stance was called *amor fati*, or "love of one's own fate." One does not wish for anything to be different because everything that happens is necessary to see what one has to see and to learn what one has to learn.

---

10 Ryan Holiday, *The Obstacle Is the Way: The Timeless Art of Turning Trials into Triumph* (Portfolio/Penguin, 2014), 56–57.

From this point of view, what some call failure others see as capital. Failure really can be an asset if what you are trying to do is improve, learn, or do something new. It is the preceding feature of nearly all successes, Holiday writes. Everything depends on perception, on exercising the ability to see differently, to change perspective and stay interested in the present. One of my fundamental errors with the fish farm was that I started seeing obstacles as learning opportunities only when the path had fully run out. With most of the challenges we faced, we did the opposite. We operated from a fixed mindset and tried to turn things around by brute force: more injection of capital, more output, more new equipment.

One of the stoic virtues is the capacity to free perception from conditioning, to understand that a single phenomenon can be viewed from many perspectives. That practice confers freedom. We are not compelled to see things as we always have or as others would like us to. Perspectives are just that, perspectives, not the absolute truth.

FRAMING

When we change our perception, we change our thoughts; with changes in thought come changes in action. This is what we, in business, call framing. Often the easiest way to solve a problem is to change how we understand it. Framing is an essential tool for tuning your mind to find opportunities.

As I mentioned in the Introduction, Robert Steven Kaplan, my former professor and author of *What to Ask the Person in the Mirror*, said that our most important story is the one about failure. We ignore that story because of a number of unconscious needs: wanting to please people and feel valuable; being limited by certain beliefs about ourselves (e.g., "I am not good enough,"

"I do not deserve any better"); and obsessing over our fears (e.g., "I had better not lose control"). Looking all of these in the face is the first step in moving from a fixed mindset to a growth one. As your new consciousness begins to develop—something I am still barely beginning—you recover part of your agency. When such reflection becomes a habit, you realize how little you know and that knowing little is not a threat but a virtue. The most successful entrepreneurs are, above all, those who welcome and enjoy doubt and uncertainty. As Kaplan says, "Successful business leaders seldom have all the answers. Instead, they are very good at knowing how and when to ask the critical questions that help them frame issues, diagnose problems, and develop action plans."[11]

Living according to that outlook is hard, especially when we are in positions of authority and our team wants to see us as sources of security and direction. But really, we are not doing any service to anyone if we are hiding our doubts and allowing others to load us down with their responsibilities.

In his book *The Gap and the Gain*, Dan Sullivan, co-founder of Strategic Coach®, offers practical tools for focusing more on the experience we already have and less on what we think we lack. Looking at what we have achieved helps us to keep our sense of purpose alive and define specific goals focused on creating value.

In his book *The Laws of Lifetime Growth*, Sullivan argues that—for someone with a growth mindset—the future is always abundant because every day offers more experience with which to face it. The ten main laws he discusses are:[12]

---

11 Robert Steven Kaplan, *What to Ask the Person in the Mirror: Critical Questions for Becoming a More Effective Leader and Reaching Your Potential* (Harvard Business Review Press, 2011), 4.

12 Dan Sullivan and Catherine Nomura, *The Laws of Lifetime Growth: Always Make Your Future Bigger Than Your Past* (Berrett-Koehler Publishers, 2006), v.

- Always make your future bigger than your past.
- Always make your learning greater than your experience.
- Always make your contribution bigger than your reward.
- Always make your performance greater than your applause.
- Always make your gratitude greater than your success.
- Always make your enjoyment greater than your effort.
- Always make your cooperation greater than your status.
- Always make your confidence greater than your comfort.
- Always make your purpose greater than your money.
- Always make your questions bigger than your answers.

I will not discuss these laws at length because they largely speak for themselves, but I highly recommend reading Sullivan's whole book.

Peter Diamandis—investor, co-founder of Singularity University, and author of several books that serve as references for me—says that the mindset from which a person operates is influenced by the five people with whom that person interacts the most.[13] Therefore, entrepreneurs who want to regularly exercise their curiosity and capacity to create value need to have contact with a community of peers and others who can question them and push them forward.

During the years when it was my responsibility to chair El Rosario's board, I was embarrassed to speak of the company and its problems. People close to me sometimes reproached me for devoting so much time and capital to a business that brought me only headaches. But after OPM, and through my connections with executives in other companies, my relationship to failure changed radically. Let's say I began to make peace with making mistakes.

13   Peter Diamandis, "Change Your Mindset, Change Your Life," Medium, September 28, 2020, https://peterhdiamandis.medium.com/change-your-mindset-change-your-life-853bd326c606.

In Colombia, and I think in Latin America generally, we are quick to judge others because there is a perception that people do not fail; rather, they are failures. A society that regards errors from that angle, from that fixed mindset, cannot progress. It is condemned to stagnate.

Errors are part of the human experience; they are a condition for growth. If we are afraid of errors, we get paralyzed, we stop acting. In cultures that judge failure harshly, people are incentivized to not-do, to not-risk, to play it safe. They prioritize protection of the ego over discovery and creativity.

That is why it is so revolutionary—at the individual, group, and even societal level—to make our relationship with failure a healthier one, to understand it as the jumping-off point for evolution. If we can frame obstacles as opportunities, we can more and more graciously accompany others who are taking risks too.

THINKING OUTSIDE THE BOX

Since my experience with El Rosario, I try to begin all my projects with the question, "Is there a way to make this work?" That is: how could this challenge be faced successfully? It sounds simple, but it is an enormous undertaking—especially when, culturally, many of us grew up doing the opposite. When we learned to seek reasons why something is impossible, why it is better not to invest energy at all.

Having the curiosity to ask this question helps us to conceive new ideas, collaborate in teams, and create value. That way, obstacles are not brakes but fuel.

At the fish farm, it was not easy to think outside the box. At least not for me. Maybe groupthink made me self-censor. I did not feel confident enough to propose risky ideas. For instance, what if instead of raising tilapia we had used the pools on the property to grow ornamental fish for exportation? That would have given us, quickly, more control over the price, and our profit margins would have been greater.

There is no use crying over spilled milk, but if I were presented now with a parcel of land with those same characteristics, I would not confine myself to its initial framing as a place to farm tilapia. I would explore other possibilities. The constant exercise of imagination is what excites me about business; not being able to put that into practice with El Rosario caused the company to feel, to me, more like a burden than an opportunity.

Soon after we liquidated the company, I began to be more disciplined about maintaining an "Is there a way to make this work?" mindset. The first challenge came at Premex, with a costly mistake that took us by surprise. We had just won back a major customer, a chicken producer who bought high volumes of our premix for feeding his animals. But one day, because of a fault in a new system we were implementing, a pigment got substituted for one of the usual components. No one noticed, and the batch went out.

Weeks later, I got a furious phone call from the customer. His hens were laying purple eggs—one million of them. Not purple on the shells, but purple inside. Although by all indications these were edible, no one wanted to see purple eggs on their tables. "What am I going to do with a million purple eggs?" the client asked me in desperation.

The first thing I did was request his pardon and assure him that we would compensate him for all the pigmented eggs, that he should not worry about the money. Then, I had to deal with the team that made the mistake.

Many people asked whether I was going to fire the person who put the wrong ingredients in the premix. Of course, I said no. The problem was what had happened, not the individual. To use that person as a scapegoat would have meant losing the opportunity for the whole team to learn.

Instead, we sat down to look for opportunities in the situation, which had cost us economically and in terms of our reputation. What did we have? We had a million purple eggs, we had machinery in our factories with the technology to transform them, we had diverse human capital, and we had a purpose of nurturing the world.

"What if we spray-dried the eggs and used them as an ingredient in protein bars, where the color does not matter?" I asked in a meeting. "What's more, that would fortify the bars with beta-carotene."

One of the team's scientists, in a fixed-mindset reflex, almost jumped out of her chair insisting this was unthinkable. The high quantity of pigment would make human consumption risky, she said.

"Really?" I asked. "You are going to reject the idea so quickly? Will you not even think about ways it could be used?"

The traditional "It won't work" conflicted with the "Can we make it work?" that the team wanted to employ. Luckily, that same scientific team found a way to spray-dry the million eggs and use the resulting powder in doses perfect for mixing with other ingredients common in protein bars on the market. In the end, our insurance company only needed to compensate us for the value of 8 percent of the million eggs; we recovered the rest from sales of the bars.

Yes, we still lost a little money, but what we learned as a team was priceless. A mistake that seemed about to cost us a fortune turned into an asset for all involved. Indeed, we finished off the whole affair of the purple eggs by applying for a patent. Now, at Iluma, this story has become synonymous with converting errors into value, with re-envisioning an obstacle as a path.

However, it is difficult to see obstacles as opportunities when you do not know where to begin. That is why I like to leverage mathematical thinking.

CHAPTER 5

LEVERAGING MATHEMATICAL THINKING

With El Rosario, my nine partners and I thought we had all the necessary ingredients to consolidate a valuable enterprise: capital, a business plan, infrastructure, raw material, and collective experience in the production of animal protein. We thought that, to grow tilapia, all we needed to consider were general factors like species genetics, water oxygenation, feed quality, pool rotation, a skilled workforce, a modern production plant, etc. But none of us took an interest in, for instance, something as simple as the temperature of the river.

Only after we were in full operation did we realize that tilapia, a warm-water species, would need more feed in the cold water of the Río Claro. Instead of needing 1.0 kilo of concentrate to yield 1.0 kilo of tilapia, we needed 1.3 kilos. Such a difference in weight may seem insignificant, but on the scale we were working, it constituted a competitive disadvantage that was both structural and decisive. If we had stuck a thermometer in the river before investing, we would surely have structured the business differently, or we would not have attempted it at all.

Another environmental variable that we did not take into account was the deforestation upstream from us. A lot of the woods that surrounded the watershed and tributaries of the Río Claro, kilometers above our property, had been cut down and replaced by coca fields. In the system we were designing to produce tilapia, deforestation was a key variable because it had a direct effect on the behavior of the river. A rainstorm in a deforested area tends to lead to sudden surges in river level like the one that carried off most of our fish.

These environmental mistakes—alongside our financial decisions and other errors—stemmed from a simplistic strategy that ignored some variables because they seemed, at first glance, to be minor. If we had taken on the task of rigorous abstraction that the investment deserved, if we had approached the challenges we faced with more curiosity and humility, we would have realized that apparently unimportant details were actually definitive factors for success. Hence the importance of examining things on a small scale.

All too often, I see companies try to solve a problem with a single stroke, without taking time to understand its complexity. Like El Rosario, they fail because they do not see how each part of a problem is connected to other parts. That is why it is so important to leverage mathematical thinking, to see problems as equations.

TREATING PROBLEMS AS EQUATIONS

As strange as it may sound, I am an entrepreneur thanks to my first girlfriend. Or, more accurately, thanks to her mother, the woman who taught me math.

If I had to choose just one of the skills that I employ every day as an entrepreneur, I would choose mathematical thinking—without a doubt. No other ability is more useful to me when it comes to creating and communicating value in a market. Mathematical thinking is my starting point for analyzing tendencies and converting data into strategy. It allows me to discover other frames of reference for reshaping problems, to create innovative products, to evaluate investment opportunities, and to optimize processes.

Unfortunately, I know many people who had bad experiences with math during their school years. They feel intimidated by numbers as a result. The same thing happened to me, until my girlfriend's mother—a brilliant systems engineer—showed me what I was missing by reducing mathematics to the formulas and rules I was made to memorize in school.

I was fifteen or sixteen when she met me and found out about my difficulty with math. "Alejo," she said, "you think you are no good with numbers, but anyone can learn. Would you like me to teach you?"

Since I wanted to spend as much time at her house as I could, having fallen in love with her daughter, I accepted the offer. After that, she taught me something new every time I visited. Within months, I was hooked. Forever.

Given my new attitude toward math, it was more or less natural that I would devote myself to business. Not because, as my father's first-born, I *had to* take on the family business, but because of enjoyment and personal vocation. Math led me to see problems as equations with several variables. To see those equations as games, as exercises of imagination, of trial and error.

VARIABLES

Another careless mistake my partners and I made with El Rosario was failing to define our variables: our clients and their needs. How can a company grow at that speed without knowing whom it is serving and how it is creating value? Nearly two years went by before we signed an agreement with a customer, and we had to drop our price because there was no one in the market who was willing to buy thousands of tilapia that had grown beyond the standard commercial size.

Now when I am faced with a proposal about a company, a new business idea, or a new product, the first thing I do is abstract the essential parts and translate them into mathematical expressions. What are the variables that influence the final answer? How are these variables related to each other?

Generally, I try to convert the facts into an equation. Here is the innovation component, there is the regulatory one, over there is the human talent; this is the financial part, that is the market challenge, this is the competitive advantage, etc. Then, as a team, we use mathematical tools to understand the nature of the problem, clarify the most important variables, and identify the levers we can use to create something unique, something that differentiates us.

At Iluma, when we are thinking about strategy, we have a mantra: "Disaggregate and deepen." That is, we break the problem down into its essential components and analyze each of them in depth. Disaggregating and deepening makes it easier to find expressions of the problem on a scale where we can have more impact or influence. Our mantra is a way of reminding ourselves of the dangers of analysis that is too wholesale, so to speak. It gives us permission to think more slowly, until we can be sure that we are considering the various subtleties of the situation.

Part of knowing your variables is having reliable information. As Mary Walton noted in her book exploring the work of management and administration theory, "In God we trust. All others must use data."[14] Trying to violate this rule is a jump into thin air. One might survive the leap, but what are the odds?

In 2016, when we decided to make our final push at El Rosario in spite of being unable to secure external investors, we confronted a very difficult fact: we had no concrete data about our inventory. We did not know exactly how many fish lived in our ponds. Our databases were just approximations.

Operationally, the method was to stock the raised ponds with alevins (tilapia fry recently hatched from eggs), but the alevins were so tiny that the only way to calculate how many were being added was to infer this from the weight of the whole batch. The margin of error could be very high. Still, this approximation was used to decide how much feed to put in a pond. Any false estimate (whether too many fish or too few) meant we were overfeeding or underfeeding the animals. Either scenario implied a loss—either a waste of feed concentrate or a delay in the fish being ready for the market.

Stocking with alevins was followed by regular sampling. Ten to thirty fish would be pulled from a pond and weighed. The average weight multiplied by the estimate of stocked alevins indicated the total fish mass in the pond.

But so many approximations often led to huge discrepancies. A pond estimated to yield thirty tons of fish at harvest could yield only twenty tons in fact. This made it hard to manage the business because basing decisions on unreliable information is like flying an airplane without instruments. Over time, it was very hard to say whether our strategy failed to produce results

---

14   Mary Walton, *The Deming Management Method* (The Berkley Publishing Group, 1986), 96.

because of this inability to measure inventory, or because there was corruption in the system, or because it was just a bad business to be in.

Mathematical thinking makes it easier to adopt scientific methods, regardless of the field of knowledge involved. For a business, the scientific method is a referent. You observe reality, ask a question, formulate a hypothetical response, investigate and gather evidence, experiment, and then analyze the data to prove or refute the initial hypothesis. Throughout the process, data and mathematical techniques are essential. I am convinced that one of the main factors causing the fish farm to end the way it did was the fuzziness of our data. However much intellect or capital we invested, there was no way to manage the business and get results.

Seeing a business problem as a multi-variable equation would have provided a useful lens to recognize complexity and prepare ourselves to meet it. Mathematical thinking trains one's apprentice eye. It suspends judgment and approaches every challenge with humility. But, having said this, I am aware that problems arise even in enterprises based on methodical and conscious planning. In those cases, it can be useful to consider systems theory.

SYSTEMS THEORY

Today, when we are interconnected in so many ways—environmentally, economically, technologically, culturally—ways of thinking can become obsolete overnight. At one time, it might have made sense to see reality as a series of isolated events, but now we have sufficient evidence that everything is interdependent.

Learning to think in systems allows us to be conscious of

complexity in ourselves and in the world we inhabit. It is, in my experience, a necessary skill for generating wealth. If we can identify the systems to which we belong, if we can recognize their goals and needs, then we can serve them better and intervene more effectively. We can become parts that are important, valuable, and hard to replace.

Systems theory, a field of study that began to take formal shape in the mid-twentieth century, is now used in many disciplines, from information technology to psychology. It offers tools and vocabulary to observe reality, abstract it into systems, and identify the points where an intervention can have the most effect. That is pure mathematical thinking, but one does not need to be a mathematician to understand the theory.

In *Thinking in Systems*, Donella H. Meadows, a researcher and professor of systems dynamics at Massachusetts Institute of Technology and Dartmouth College, popularized the theory while limiting equations to an appendix at the end. She explains: "When a systems thinker encounters a problem, the first thing he or she does is look for data, time graphs, the history of the system. That's because long-term behavior provides clues to the underlying system structure. And structure is the key to understanding not just what is happening, but why."[15]

A company gains competitive advantage from being able to analyze systemic causes of what is happening inside it. Graphs of behavior over time—whether in the realm of finance, sales, production, etc.—reveal whether the firm is reaching its limit or whether there is a vein that still offers potential for growth. It is not possible to determine this by following just one vari-

---

15   Donella H. Meadows, *Thinking in Systems: A Primer*, ed. Diana Wright (Chelsea Green Publishing, 2008), 89.

able over time. Rather, it is necessary to follow a broader set of variables defined by the complexity of the system.

At El Rosario, not having this ability exhausted us. We lived in reaction mode, dousing one fire after another without examining how the structure of the organization itself made us more vulnerable to what I call "the ten plagues." Although we had reasonably good data, especially about things that could be quantified, we did not want to hear what the information was shouting at us. The business lost money for structural reasons, and everything we invested flowed into operating costs and debt payments. We thought we just needed time—so many companies, after all, lose money for years before becoming profitable—but systemic analysis said something different.

Another advantage of systems thinking is that it changes how we understand responsibility. I grew up in a culture that tends to explain deficiency or dysfunction psychologically. If a goal is not achieved, that is the responsibility of this person for being distracted, of that person for being reckless, of the other person for being selfish. In systems thinking, any individual characteristic forms part of the system. Instead of assigning responsibility to individuals, you study the conditions that allow certain traits to be amplified or suppressed. You study the conditions that lead to decisions being made against the interests of the system as a whole.

One key concept in systems theory is "limited rationality." That is, people make rational decisions based on the information they have. The problem is that they often make those decisions while operating in parts of the system where not enough information arrives. So, however rational the individual's decision seems, it may be irrational for the system. And blaming an individual or replacing him or her with someone else is no solution: the replacement will probably suffer from the same lack of information. In such circumstances—like when we went from one managing director to another at El Rosario—what is needed is to review the intrinsic responsibility of the system.

"'Intrinsic responsibility,'" Meadows writes, "means that the system is designed to send feedback about the consequences of decision making directly and quickly and compellingly to the decision makers."[16] How well does information flow through the system? What are the incentives for each part to be monitoring and communicating the impact of overall decisions? In the end, understanding responsibility as a systemic property, not that of one individual or team, allows for a deeper analysis of the condition of the business. Over the long run, that saves a lot of energy.

What is interesting about what happened at El Rosario is not the chain of misfortunes but how the system responded to them. A systems lens reveals that we were responsible for the problems that faced the company, although that is not how we saw it at the time. Understanding this concept can multiply the value created by a company, as well as reduce anxiety and stress.

As I write this book now, the global economy is at an inflection point. Central bank interest rates have been rising constantly for a year with the goal of taming inflation, and the pressure of political and financial systems on companies is becoming an existential challenge. Until six months ago, an Iluma product could be viable if it brought a return equal to or greater than 7 percent. But now, what is required is 20 percent. Many companies have gone under because they cannot quickly adapt to the pressure.

At Iluma, to become more efficient without falling into the

---

16   Meadows, *Thinking in Systems*, 179.

trap of uncontrolled price increases, we decided on a general restructuring of our alliance. One of the first proposed solutions was to reassign the roles in our management team. That could result in optimization, yes, but it would not allow for having conversations about systemic issues.

Organizations must restructure themselves backward, toward the client. That is, they must ask, what is the value we create? What is the differentiation we can offer to clients? Why do we matter to them? Those questions allow us to identify company outcomes that—although it is disturbing to recognize this—are irrelevant to the market. Those irrelevant outcomes are what we have begun to eliminate, and in the process, we have discovered how many human and material resources we had invested in ideas, projects, and other things that had little value.

To reconfigure the system from that perspective—from the final interests of the customer—makes it both better and leaner. But to do that in a responsible way, it is indispensable to follow some principles of systems thinking, and to use mathematical models of the organization to guide modifications and adjustments.

The mathematician Terence Tao, citing Vladimir Arnold, said that math is the part of science that allows for experimenting most cheaply.[17] Abstracting the system, understanding businesses as multi-variable equations, allows you to make adjustments and calculate their effects (or at least approximating them) using only computer software or pencils and paper. This practice has served me well.

---

17 Terence Tao, *Structure and Randomness: Pages from Year One of a Mathematical Blog* (American Mathematical Society, 2008), 203.

TRANSFORMING LIMITATIONS INTO OPPORTUNITIES

In 2000, when Adiquim—the first company I directed—was in a phase of steady expansion, we came up against a problem. We had found the right formula for creating a scarce and valuable product for the market, but we did not have a way to convert it to powdered form. The few companies that made similar products used spray dryers to pulverize the material, but those machines cost a fortune that we could not yet pay.

One possible solution was to use a form of silica that would absorb the liquid, but that would not work because the material remained damp. Then it occurred to us to try something that was apparently absurd. Nearby our plant was a bakery—what if we put the damp silica in one of their ovens, dried it, and then milled that mass to turn it into powder?

We tried this out, almost as a joke. To our surprise, it worked perfectly. We ended up buying a bakery oven at a fraction of the cost of a spray dryer. We were able to offer the market a product that matched our competitors in quality. When asked how we managed to do this without spray dryers, we smiled as if we were protecting the formula for Coca-Cola.

A given mathematical problem can be solved in many different ways. Every initial challenge begins a process of discovery that can yield an elegant solution in just a few steps or demand a long odyssey before reaching the end. Becoming comfortable with uncertainty is a part of the method.

If anything trains one in mathematical thinking, it is resourcefulness: making use of what one has. Startups and the most innovative companies are those that recognize their restrictions and take the risk of confronting large problems in spite of them. Along the way, they often create something unexpected and valuable.

Necessity is the mother of invention, and a virtuoso entrepreneur can transform limitations into opportunities to innovate. I am not saying mathematics is indispensable for this process, but it definitely provides great training. Mathematical thinking not only offers useful tools for analyzing the daily problems confronted by entrepreneurs, it also cultivates a more curious and open-minded attitude in the face of adversity. However, as I will show in the next chapter, math cannot solve everything; that is why it is crucial to pay attention to the winds of change.

CHAPTER 6

PAY ATTENTION TO THE WINDS OF CHANGE

In 2015, El Rosario's last director said we were using obsolete technology, and if we did not update our methods, there was no way to increase production. He recommended installing special aerators for the ponds so that the tilapia would need less food and would grow faster, but the investment would be half a million dollars.

We decided to take the risk, but this time I also decided to keep a much closer watch on what was going on. I asked both my personal assistant and one of the best financial analysts at Premex to devote half of their work time to El Rosario. When the financial analyst began going over the figures, he confirmed what an outside firm had told us during our search for new investors: El Rosario's assets and liabilities totaled zero. Yet according to the projections we made after restructuring the business to increase production, in only a few years we would be able to repay our debt and reach the breakeven point.

When we installed the aerators, a new cycle began. For

the first time in years, the fish farm began to show results. We lowered our costs and increased our output and sales. We were excited to find that it was indeed possible to do things differently.

But then tilapia began dying of a virus. Once again, morning would find the surface of the ponds littered with thousands and thousands of lifeless fish. That was the end of the fragile enthusiasm we had regained.

As if the virus was not enough, the director called me one day to report something even worse. He said that one of our neighbors, a local environmental leader, was mobilizing communities to oppose the company. This leader charged that our operation was polluting the river, producing a noxious odor downstream, and negatively affecting the ecotourism that makes the Río Claro one of the most-visited natural areas in Colombia.

We had carried out strict inspections and complied with all environmental regulations, but the smear campaign was for real. Within weeks, there was an online petition asking the authorities to prevent the "debacle" that, according to the signers, we were unleashing:

The discharge of waste from the processing plant (piscícola El Rosario) is polluting and degrading this water source (Río Claro), a tourist attraction in Antioquia. You should demand and require the owners of this plant to properly manage and deposit those wastes without contaminating the river or other environments.

Thousands of people signed the petition. Now, in addition to the financial and operational pressures we already had to confront, we were facing social pressure too.

To act impartially, we turned to outside institutions to review our impact on the ecosystem. One of the country's most prestigious universities did a study and found that the plant's impact was minimal and within legal limits. But the pressure did not abate.

In 2017, the managing director called me again and told me there was something he had to give me in person. He came to my office with an envelope in hand and a funeral expression on his face, saying that the attorney general had opened a case to investigate us, on the presumption we had been polluting.

I was not concerned because we already had certificates of compliance from the environmental authorities, a university study, and internal inspection documents. But when I consulted one of the country's best environmental attorneys the next day, his opinion was alarming: "Look, Alejandro, there is a law that covers environmental damage. You can be in compliance with all the current regulations, but if the attorney general can show that El Rosario provoked or is provoking any irreparable damage—no matter when—you personally are responsible. And since this is in the criminal code, it can mean prison time."

Prison. The mere idea left me silent. I have always behaved responsibly, never swindled anyone, never stolen a dime, yet me, in prison... No way was it worth the risk. If I needed a reason to let go of El Rosario completely—something I should have done years before—this was definitely it.

I decided to meet with the local environmental leader, the one who had publicly expressed his concern about the fish farm's impact. The director had described him to me as a monster, someone motivated more by envy than by a genuine interest in protecting the river. To my surprise, I met a well-intentioned human being, straightforward and approachable. I toured the area with him, and he showed me some changes in the ecosystem that could not be directly attributed to the fish farm but that unsettled him nonetheless.

It was a tense meeting, but we seemed to understand each other. Like that environmental leader, I am aware that we must not do damage to the planet we depend on. His work seemed admirable to me.

It became clear that at El Rosario, we made the mistake of not reading the Zeitgeist (pronounced tsight-guy-st), a German concept referring to the spirit of the times. The invisible force that shapes the characteristics of an era. I consider the Zeitgeist key because it recognizes that we are not isolated subjects; there is something that incentivizes us to form relationships and build together. If, as an entrepreneur, you do not tune your sensibility to identify the spirit of the time in which you live, your talents and efforts are less likely to be valued.

The prevailing winds of our time tell us, more clearly every day, that there is no way to amplify our energy if we do so to the detriment of the planet and its ecosystems. Economic development cannot outrun stewardship of the environment.

At El Rosario, our problem was not that we created a fish farm—aquaculture is an efficient and necessary source of animal protein—but where we created it. Our production depended on water from a river that ran through our land, and no matter how rigorous we were about meeting the legal environmental standards, we were putting more complexity into an ecosystem already made fragile by other human pressures.

I think the Zeitgeist is something that is felt much more easily than it can be articulated or defined. It is uncertain, and it depends on so many variables that attempting to label it is futile. It is so subtle that even attempting to observe it causes it to change.

However, there are aspects of the Zeitgeist that do stand out, and we can take these into consideration as we align our efforts with the times. In this chapter, I want to explore some of these aspects, how we can see them as opportunities to renew our relationship with the planet and thereby create value.

REPAIRING THE WORLD

The summons from the attorney general was an alarm bell. In hindsight, we should not have waited until then to understand that our operations in Río Claro represented a potential environmental risk that would in no way be offset by the value we hoped to create. But we were living in a period of transition between Zeitgeists, during which we came to realize (much more slowly than necessary) that the industrial model based on exploitation of nature is not viable in the long run. Many of the blows we received—storms, droughts, viruses, etc.—were signals that we were setting up a confrontation with nature. Nothing good comes out of that.

For a long time, "sustainability" has been held aloft as a goal, as a hallmark of environmental commitment. But I think we have arrived at a point when sustainability is not enough. The Jewish concept Tikkun Olam is more apt for this moment.

With roots in the Kabbalah, Tikkun Olam means "repairing the world" and refers to acts such as promoting social justice or environmental healing. It is our responsibility to improve the world during our passage through it, to support regeneration.

Regeneration is a complex challenge for those of us working in the agricultural-nutritional sector. It implies meeting two needs that we have seen as polar opposites: the health of the planet and feeding a growing world population. The irony is, there is no way to produce food out of a sick earth, yet we are the inheritors of a system that looks at the interests of humanity as if they were independent of the interests of other species.

Fortunately, that viewpoint is changing. Consciousness of

human interdependence with our ecosystem is now a part of the Zeitgeist.

THE ANTHROPOCENE

Many scientists say we have entered the Anthropocene, a new geologic epoch in which human pressures have a mounting and destabilizing impact on the planet.[18] Recognizing the Anthropocene is recognizing the power we hold that has gotten out of hand, but also recognizing our power to cure and reimagine our relationship with what surrounds us.

What systems of production will be valued and rewarded in the Anthropocene? I think it will be those that contribute to the regeneration of the earth, its ecosystem, and the well-being of both humans and animals. The challenge is to develop a productive model that can meet our needs without deforestation, without contaminating the air or the rivers, without uprooting mountains. A model of a virtuous cycle, even if we find it uncomfortable and even if it poses a personal and social challenge.

Making room for complexity is one of the abilities that I try to cultivate. I think it has served me in getting through the uncertainty of this historical moment, in navigating the unknown.

Even though the urgency of regeneration is clear, we continue to depend on fossil fuels and on minerals that come from irregular mining or overfishing. We have trespassed beyond the limits of the earth's resilience, yet the effects of suddenly

---

18 Will Steffen et al., "The Anthropocene: Are Humans Now Overwhelming the Great Forces of Nature?," *Ambio* 36, no. 8 (December 2007): 614–621, https://doi.org/10.1579/0044-7447(2007)36[614:TAAHNO]2.0.CO;2.

bringing the current system to a halt would be as disastrous as those of prolonging it indefinitely. That is the complexity that hurts, but that also inspires: recognizing that in spite of the damage we are doing, we have the energy, knowledge, mindset, technology, and innovation to develop alternative models. Otherwise, any effort to contribute to regeneration will be in vain. The current problems will grow worse, damaging our mental, physical, and emotional health.

The aquaculture experience taught me the need to listen to nature before investing energy and resources into a seemingly productive project that affects an ecosystem. This means we have to leave our egos at the door, to understand that we are on earth temporarily and that we are only one tiny part of an extensive and complex system.

A guiding question can be: does the operation under consideration allow future generations to continue cherishing and benefitting from the land that is involved? The fish farm did not pass that test. The area where it was located, I can see clearly now, is more valuable as a space for conservation and ecological tourism than as a base for the industry we tried to set up.

THE INFORMATION ERA

El Rosario was a company that used two traditional levers to generate wealth: capital and labor. We had more than a hundred employees, and we invested millions of dollars in infrastructure, machinery, inputs, training, etc., to cultivate and sell a product that would net us a large return. But capital and labor are not such powerful levers in the current Zeitgeist. In the information era, managing people or managing enormous sums of capital is not indispensable to creating wealth.

Investor Naval Ravikant defines wealth as having "assets

that earn while you sleep."[19] That is, assets that grow over time without us having to put in more. To create wealth today, he says, the most powerful lever is products that multiply without marginal cost. In other words, products that can be distributed via information technology, especially of the digital variety. He continues:[20]

> This was only invented in the last few hundred years. It started with the printing press. It accelerated with broadcast media, and now it's really blown up with the internet and with coding. Now, you can multiply your efforts without involving other humans and without needing money from other humans.

According to Ravikant, the information era technology manifests in two specific ways: through software coding or programming and through digital content. Anyone who knows how to program or to produce valuable information for distribution over the internet has an advantageous position in the market. I would add another category: patents. Those who own patents have an asset that can exponentially amplify the effort that was required to develop them.

A key characteristic of this new way to generate value via information technology is that it disconnects input from output. The value-added does not depend on the number of hours of work but on good judgment, originality, and individual talent. In general, this new disconnect of input and output is most likely to appear in the kinds of work that offer more room for creativity. A single line of brilliant code, an influential

19 Eric Jorgenson, *The Almanack of Naval Ravikant: A Guide to Wealth and Happiness* (Magrathea Publishing, 2020), 38.

20 Jorgenson, *The Almanack*, 59.

podcast, a viral song or TikTok can generate more wealth than a year of ordinary work.

Furthermore, Ravikant says, information technology can be utilized without anyone's permission or authorization.[21]

> For labor leverage, somebody has to decide to follow you. For capital leverage, somebody has to give you money to invest or to turn into a product.

> Coding, writing books, recording podcasts, tweeting, YouTubing—these kinds of things are permissionless. You don't need anyone's permission to do them, and that's why they are very egalitarian. They're great equalizers of leverage.

One of the most admired abilities in the business world is that of identifying the points within a system where an intervention will have the greatest impact. In the current Zeitgeist, that skill is directly connected with a precise grasp of information and its flows, which are now more democratic than ever. What is the information the system needs to open new possibilities? What information is hiding in plain sight, without anyone having taken advantage of it? How can oceans of information be translated into practical and transformative knowledge?

In *The Information: A History, A Theory, A Flood*, science journalist James Gleick argues that in the information era there are two abilities that bring the highest rewards: filtering and searching.[22] Those who develop filtering tools (like the Amazon

---

21   Jorgenson, *The Almanack*, 60.

22   James Gleick, *The Information: A History, a Theory, a Flood* (Pantheon Books, 2011), 411.

algorithm) or tools that help us seek information (Google) have more power to generate value.

At Asimetrix, one of Iluma's companies, we capture information from farms and ranches in real time, filter it, cross-reference it, and convert it into useful knowledge for the producers. Our service translates what is going on at the farm into programming language so that computers can help us distill large and flexible volumes of apparently isolated data into personalized knowledge and profit. It quickly analyzes data and spots improbable linkages between productivity, efficiency, and the regeneration of the earth and animal welfare.

Thanks to the hundreds of variables related to animal health that we have been able to measure, we have designed early interventions for when the system of sensors warns that an outbreak of disease is highly probable. We are also experimenting and advancing in the development of alternatives to antibiotics so that antibiotic use can be restricted to emergency cases.

One of my frustrations with El Rosario was that we had so little information—and of such poor quality—on which to base decisions. Also, as I have mentioned, this was a business built on efficiency, on minutiae, in which the available data was used for, more than anything else, optimizing processes rather than creating new goods or services. Today, I select and devote myself to businesses in which information is abundant and is used as a creative tool. These are businesses that allow for blending data with imagination, so as to explore and create what does not yet exist.

ARTIFICIAL INTELLIGENCE

So-called artificial intelligence has dominated worldwide conversation of late. "AI" is without a doubt a force that will mold our Zeitgeist and that of coming generations, but I do not call it *intelligence*. It is *machine learning*, a powerful technology that uses statistical techniques and databases to produce results similar to human language and thought. Despite this technology's potential to help us via analysis of complex and far-flung webs of information, I think it is a mistake to assume that such huge language models will replace human beings in the creation of knowledge.

Machine learning technologies can describe and predict scenarios, but the more training data they receive, the more their algorithms tend to converge. In those conditions, their results cut off the tails of the curves. They veer away from information at the margins, from the information that differentiates. Without differentiation, there is no value. The more people use this technology, and the more democratic it is, the more it will resemble a perfect market, a herd market in which no one wins because everyone is offering the same thing.

The creation of value takes place in a more mysterious way, almost always through mental processes that machine learning cannot replicate. Value is not produced so much by prediction as by explaining phenomena: discovering improbable rules like the logic that underlies thinking or natural laws like gravity, the equations of electromagnetic phenomena, the potential of a fungus to cure diseases, etc. In sum, the value that changes things and creates progress, the value that makes a difference, tends to be found through serendipity and through processes that are not always tied to the linearity of language.

In his book *How Innovation Works*, writer Matt Ridley explores this topic in depth:[23]

> Innovations come in many forms, but one thing they all have in common, and which they share with biological innovations created by evolution, is that they are enhanced forms of improbability. That is to say, innovations, be they iPhones, ideas or eider ducklings, are all unlikely, improbable combinations of atoms and digital bits of information...Innovation, then, means finding new ways to apply energy to create improbable things, and see them catch on. It means much more than invention, because the word implies developing an invention to the point where it catches on because it is sufficiently practical, affordable, reliable and ubiquitous to be worth using.

To create differentiated value requires thinking. Technologies of so-called artificial intelligence can catalyze thought but cannot replace it. They are designed to find the word, the sentence, the paragraph with the greatest probability of following the one before.

Innovation operates under different rules, rules that require freedom, experimentation, trial and error. Rigorously thinking of philosophy as experience, not just words, enables you to find opportunities to create what no one else can. This is the basis of any worthwhile business. Of course, once a new and different idea appears, machine learning technologies can be very effective levers for helping to scale it up, to amplify it.

---

23   Matt Ridley, *How Innovation Works: And Why It Flourishes in Freedom* (Harper, 2020), 2–4.

HOMO RETICULARIS

The technologies we use to communicate model the societies we live in. That was one of the central insights of the mid-twentieth-century theorist Marshall McLuhan: the medium is the message.[24] More important than the information we transmit is understanding how we are transmitting it. The world in which ideas and stories circulated via singing bards or hand-written manuscripts was radically different from the world of the printing press or of mass communication technologies like radio or television.

The fact that today we communicate mainly over the internet, a global computer network, is revolutionizing the ways we relate. Our bodies, identities, and behaviors are being digitized. The internet has helped to create communities that would have been unthinkable a generation ago. That new ability—a fundamental marker of our Zeitgeist—is opening the way for what some call "homo reticularis," or individuals who are part of a society that features cooperation and creativity through informatic networks. These networks are not limited by geography, and everyone within them can produce and consume information on a large scale.

Learning to maneuver in networks is key for creating value. And to do that, we have to modernize our way of seeing the world. We are no longer limited to the human talent available in a local market. The market is worldwide, and those who know how to connect with the resources available in the global network have a structural advantage over their competitors.

Awareness of homo reticularis changed my paradigm of possibilities. Now we can have contractors in the Philippines, research underway in the United States, and important

---

24   Marshall McLuhan, *Understanding Media: The Extensions of Man* (McGraw-Hill, 1964), 7.

customers in Japan. Those networks of cooperation, if well designed and supported by international regulation, not only open avenues for growth but also add unique and differentiated value to what we produce. Although, of course, we must keep in mind that every culture has its own patterns of collaboration; therefore, the learning curve early in the relationship is very steep.

There are two indispensable conditions for cooperating in a network in which we do not know the person on the other side of the communication, the one who is offering the goods or services. The first condition is integrity: although it is easy to betray someone else's confidence when operating within a system with minimal legal consequences (a judge in Colombia has no jurisdiction over an engineer in Poland, for example) it is probable that the same network would take charge of expelling or neutralizing those who do not meet responsibilities. Without integrity, opportunities to connect productive or creative communities are significantly reduced.

The other condition is humility: the networks exist precisely because those participating in them openly recognize their limitations (in knowledge, technical capacities, technology, etc.) and know that cooperation creates value for all involved. Statements like "I do not know, and that is why I need you" equalize relationships and allow different nodes of the network to join in a common purpose. They can then devote themselves to the thing that makes them most distinct and valuable.

Some years ago, at Iluma, we posed a question: whom would we invite to join an advisory board to better understand the future of the nutritional industry? Many of the suggested names belonged to experts spread over several continents who had no relations with each other. We got in touch with them, explained our history and our mission, and all but one agreed to travel and meet us in person to contribute their experience and knowledge to what we were building.

Besides integrity and humility, homo reticularis respects the law of reciprocity. Reciprocity is the very first lever mentioned by social psychologist Robert Cialdini when he speaks about the ways in which a person can amplify his or her influence in a network.[25] There is no way to create value in a network if the relationships among its members are seen as a zero-sum game, one in which some win and others lose. Networks are systems that are nourished and grow if the generation of wealth is reciprocal.

Iluma is an alliance just for this reason. Though each business is independent and has a distinct focus, all are guided by the purpose of creating a better-nourished world, and all benefit from the output of the others.

Homo reticularis—whether as an individual or a society—is motivated by a clear goal and by the consciousness of what makes this species unique. Those characteristics make it easier to interact with other nodes of the network that share interests and derive mutual benefit from the relationship. Paradoxically, interdependence makes each of the parts more sovereign in itself.

To conclude, the concept of homo reticularis has helped me gain a clearer understanding of market asymmetries. Statistician Nassim Taleb describes asymmetries as the irregular distribution of risks and rewards in a system or network.[26] There are processes that can be carried out in two different parts of the world, but the downside of doing them in one part can be much greater than that of doing them in another part.

For instance, there are chemical reagents that, for use in

25   Robert B. Cialdini, *Influence: The Psychology of Persuasion* (Collins, 2007), 17–56.

26   Nassim Nicholas Taleb, *Antifragile: Things That Gain from Disorder* (Random House, 2012), 35.

Colombia, require a lot of bureaucratic permissions, from approval by national cabinet ministries to authorizations from anti-drug agents. Yet that same reagent can be bought with three clicks in the United States. That asymmetry, which seems insignificant, can cost millions on an industrial scale, so it makes sense to carry out the process where the downside is less. To work in networks so that everyone can survive, expand, and grow stronger.

TUNING IN TO THE ZEITGEIST

I do not believe that sensing the Zeitgeist requires any particular action, just as no thinking is required to make the heart beat or the sun rise. The spirit of the time motivates and molds individuals and cultures, whether we like it or not. What we can do, though, is focus our attention so that we can recognize the Zeitgeist's manifestations for what they are.

I have personally found conversation to be a practice that makes me better acquainted with the force that shapes our time. As I mentioned earlier, at Iluma we believe that we are how we talk, so we intentionally encourage spaces for spontaneous conversation among people from different teams within the organization. Such conversations give rise to the most valuable knowledge in our ecosystem of companies. We learn or realize what we are doing, where those activities came from, how they have cross-pollinated, and where new opportunities to create value are opening up. As Alejandro Salazar points out in his book *The Emergent Strategy: And the Death of Strategic Planning*, the strategy of a business is, essentially, a conversation.[27]

---

27   Alejandro Salazar, *The Emergent Strategy: And the Death of Strategic Planning* (Emergent Strategy, 2024), 14.

Reclaiming Conversation, by MIT professor Sherry Turkle, is a key book for understanding the importance of conversation and how scarce it has become in societies where more and more interaction takes place through digital platforms:[28]

> This new mediated life has gotten us into trouble. Face-to-face conversation is the most human—and humanizing—thing we do. Fully present to one another, we learn to listen. It's where we develop the capacity for empathy. It's where we experience the joy of being heard, of being understood. And conversation advances self-reflection, the conversations with ourselves that are the cornerstone of early development and continue throughout life...Without conversation, studies show that we are less empathic, less connected, less creative and fulfilled. We are diminished, in retreat.

Turkle is right to connect conversation with individual reflection. I think it is through the practice of learning to listen to others and to oneself that the outlines of the Zeitgeist appear. Deep listening—sometimes alone and sometimes in a group—allows for taking some distance, widening the lens, and refreshing perceptions. That is when our most deeply rooted assumptions, those things that seem obvious or that we most take for granted, can be questioned and transformed.

Another advantage of conversation, Turkle argues, is that it allows us to discover and communicate what makes each of us unique, each of us different: "The best way to avoid being seen as a commodity is to offer a relationship. And that takes conversation...If you can't differentiate yourself, then all this

---

28   Sherry Turkle, *Reclaiming Conversation: The Power of Talk in a Digital Age* (Penguin Books, 2015), 3, 13.

technology just makes us go faster, but it kind of makes us anonymous; it makes us all the same."[29]

Conversation helps to cultivate attention, to quiet the cacophony of automatic thinking and surprise ourselves with the outlook of the other person. It is a way of, for a moment, being that other person—identifying needs and values that may be foreign to us so that we can serve or support them.

One of the risks facing those who manage companies is that we disconnect from reality by limiting conversation to the level of executives close to us. However specific the reports of vice presidents or leaders may be, nothing replaces direct conversation with members of the team. The fable of the emperor's new clothes—where the entire court is afraid to tell the naked emperor the truth—is a fine warning about the importance of keeping conversations open with all stakeholders, including critics, competitors, and detractors.

One of the main lessons I learned from the last years of the aquaculture company is that it is better not to take the word of third parties because some conflicts can be resolved only through direct conversations. According to one of the managing directors of El Rosario, the local environmental leader who was carrying out a campaign against our operations "did not have good intentions, but just wanted to stir up the community for his own benefit." At first, I believed the director, but after speaking directly with the leader, I realized I had been given a distorted impression. This neighbor was someone to talk with, someone I should have listened to many years before the problems arose.

To close this chapter, I want to highlight the value of leisure as a means to connect with the spirit of the time. I appreciate

---

29 Turkle, *Reclaiming Conversation*, 288.

moments and activities with no purpose other than to be present. I value them not only as a break from the daily grind of work, but also because they refresh my outlook and oxygenate my creativity.

For me, leisure takes many forms. I try to consume a steady diet of readings, documentaries, and feature films; to go to concerts; to travel with my family or friends; to take walks in nature and surprise myself with unexpected encounters. And what frequently happens is that suddenly, when I am supposedly doing nothing, when I am giving myself over to the present moment, new ideas pop up or I spot possible solutions to problems I have been thinking about for a long time. I am not saying that being more productive should be the goal of leisure, but I appreciate that when the mind is not being motivated by incentives or rewards, it is open to lessons and new ways of seeing things.

It is getting harder and harder to disconnect ourselves and enjoy leisure. Paradoxically, it requires discipline to stop working, let go of screens, and cultivate "doing nothing." Nonetheless, in order to create value, the ideal is to balance activity and contemplation, producing and resting. I think that learning how to oscillate along that spectrum is one of the things our Zeitgeist is inviting us to do.

Unfortunately, when you fail to recognize the Zeitgeist in time, as we did with El Rosario, you may be left with the responsibility of closing your company. In that case, try to negotiate so everybody wins.

CHAPTER 7

NEGOTIATE SO EVERYBODY WINS

In June 2017, nine years after El Rosario's first meeting, my father and I met with the rest of our partners at the creative center of Premex in Medellín—a spacious, well-lit boardroom dominated by an enormous photo of Steve Jobs. "Señores," I said, "I am done. Today is my last day with El Rosario."

At first, they tried to dissuade me. "We cannot bail out now," one of the partners said with alarm. Then he played the card we already knew too well: "Just one more push will get us to the breakeven point."

"In that case," I replied, "we will compensate the rest of you for our part of the debt, and we will give you our shares so you can keep the company going. But we will not continue being part of it."

That was a sincere offer. The downside confronting us was reason enough for us to get out, but if the other partners still believed the fish farm had a future, neither my family nor I would get in their way.

However, when I told our partners about the attorney general's summons and the risk implied for everyone, they understood there was no other way. We hired an attorney who specialized in liquidations to guide us through the process of creating a proposal that we could present to the bank. I then took on the most uncomfortable task, which was negotiating our debt with the bank.

The goal was to arrange things so that the debt payments would, to the extent possible, not damage the businesses that each of us had outside of El Rosario. After all, we were all going to lose millions of dollars. We were already going through every stage of grief.

During these negotiations, I witnessed what happens when people are pushed to the max. That process, which lasted for months and took up at least 80 percent of my time and energy, taught me that closing companies requires as much care as opening them.

CLOSING A COMPANY CAREFULLY

In *Negotiating the Impossible*, Deepak Malhotra—an expert with decades of experience negotiating in political, business, and scientific environments—says:[30]

> I find that I am at my best when I remain mindful of the fact that negotiation, regardless of the context or stakes, is about human interaction. When you're dealing with human beings, you should bring the best of what it means to be human. If you can balance assertiveness with empathy, self-confidence with the humility necessary to learn and adapt, and the desire to influence with a genuine interest in understanding, you will be in great shape. The rest is corollaries and details.

---

30 Deepak Malhotra, *Negotiating the Impossible: How to Break Deadlocks and Resolve Ugly Conflicts (Without Money or Muscle)* (Berrett-Koehler, 2016), 198.

He goes on to say that to be a good negotiator does not require having capital or power or imposing one's will on the other party. Instead of using force, he recommends focusing on three elements that appear in any negotiation and are key to capturing the greatest possible value from the matter at hand: (1) framing (i.e., what are we negotiating about?), (2) process (i.e., how are we going to negotiate?), and (3) empathy (i.e., who is across the table, and what do they care about?).

Malhotra suggests that the first step in a negotiation is trying to control the frame of reference. He says it is important to be clear not only about what you are going to propose, but also about the form in which you will propose it. Whoever defines the viewpoint or lens from which the problem will be observed has an advantage in the process:[31]

> The "frame" of the negotiation is a psychological lens. It is a sense-making apparatus that influences how people perceive each other, the issues at hand, and the options that exist... Regardless of the objective stakes, much of what determines how people approach a problem depends on how they (or their constituents) subjectively make sense of it.

That all sounds good, and surely anyone who reads that passage with a cool head will agree with it. But the reality is much more complicated. It was not easy for each of us to bring to the table "the best of what it means to be human" when our egos were wounded and we stood to lose quite a few zeroes.

In our case, we needed the regional officers of the bank to understand that this was not just one more liquidation process. Our goal was for them to see El Rosario as a company

---

31 Malhotra, *Negotiating the Impossible*, 11–12.

with a unique mission—efficiently producing animal protein and generating employment in a neglected geographic area—which had marshaled the leadership and effort of ten of the most renowned entrepreneurs of the region but which faced structural challenges that were outside our control. We needed an honorable way out because the majority of the partners had profitable businesses that were clients of the bank.

We wanted to make sure, at all costs, that the closing of the fish farm would not affect our capacity to create value—in our other businesses, in the society as a whole, and as a consequence, for the bank. If we could get the bank to understand that it was in their interest to work closely with us during this unfortunate process, so as to continue capturing a share of the value of what we did outside El Rosario, then the negotiation would be off to a good start. That was the story we wanted to tell, so we prepared ourselves to tell it.

THE PRISONER'S DILEMMA

Some partners suggested a more hostile approach to the negotiations, but I resisted. There is powerful data demonstrating that people who are generous and pleasant at the beginning of a negotiation tend to get better results in the long run.

That may sound counterintuitive because a deeply rooted cultural paradigm holds that the best negotiator is the one with the most resources to dominate the other—through strength, cleverness, or deception. The idea of coming to the table with goodwill, with equal concern for one's own interest and for the interest of one's counterpart, sounds naive at best. However, in 1979, a political scientist named Robert Axelrod did an experiment to understand the logic of human cooperation and discover what generates more individual benefit.[32] Is it action motivated by selfishness and personal interest, or is it action motivated by achieving reciprocal benefit?

Axelrod based his experiment on game theory, a branch of mathematics that studies the behavior of networks in which the optimum decision of one actor depends on the behavior and decisions of others. At the time, the conversation among social scientists assumed that humans are essentially selfish, so it seemed paradoxical that a species of selfish individuals should have prospered from cooperation. The cooperation seemed illogical, but still it was a definitive and constant aspect of humanity.

That dilemma was formulated mathematically in game theory in the 1950s, and soon was dubbed "the prisoner's dilemma." In the book called *The Origins of Virtue*, Matt Ridley summarizes the game:[33]

> The game is called the prisoner's dilemma because the commonest anecdote to illustrate it describes two prisoners each faced with the choice of giving evidence against the other and so reducing his own sentence. The dilemma arises because if neither defects on the other, the police can convict them both only on a lesser charge, so both would be better off if they stayed silent, but each is individually better off if he defects.

> Why? Forget prisoners and think of it as a simple mathematical game you play with another player for points. If

---

32 Robert Axelrod, *The Evolution of Cooperation* (Basic Books, 1984), 27–54.

33 Matt Ridley, *The Origins of Virtue: Human Instincts and the Evolution of Cooperation* (Penguin Books, 1996), 54.

you both cooperate ("stay silent") you each get three (this is called the "reward"); if you both defect you each get one (the "punishment"). But if one defects and the other cooperates, the cooperator gets nothing (the "sucker's pay-off") and the defector gets five points (the "temptation"). So, if your partner defects, you are better off defecting, too. That way you get one point rather than none. But if your partner cooperates, you are still better off defecting: you get five instead of three. Whatever the other person does, you are better off defecting. Yet, since he argues the same way, the certain outcome is mutual defection: one point each, when you could have had three each.

What Axelrod did was digitize the game. He invited scientists from various disciplines to design computer programs that would play "the prisoner's dilemma." Each program would have its own particular rules (e.g., always defect, alternate cooperation with defection, defect on the one who always cooperates). They would play two hundred rounds against the other programs, against themselves, and against one other program chosen at random. At the end, the points would be counted and a winner declared.

The undisputed winner was a very simple program called Tit-for-tat. That program (or rule) begins by always cooperating and then goes on to do whatever its opponent did in the previous round: if the opponent cooperated, so does Tit-for-tat; if the opponent defects, it defects too. But once revenge is taken, it again displays its inclination to cooperate.

Axelrod published the results in a book called *The Evolution of Cooperation*. One of the most surprising outcomes was that the eight best-performing programs all began with an inclination to cooperate, not to defect or try to take advantage of the opponent. In other words, all the programs were "nice." At the end of the chapter about this simulation, Axelrod describes why the rules of Tit-for-tat favor mutual power:[34]

> What accounts for Tit-for-tat's robust success is its combination of being nice, retaliatory, forgiving, and clear. Its niceness prevents it from getting into unnecessary trouble. Its retaliation discourages the other side from persisting whenever defection is tried. Its forgiveness helps restore mutual cooperation. And its clarity makes it intelligible to the other player, thereby eliciting long-term cooperation.

He also includes an observation that is important for anyone preparing to negotiate:[35]

> Even expert strategists from political science, sociology, economics, psychology, and mathematics made the systematic errors of being too competitive for their own good, not being forgiving enough, and being too pessimistic about the responsiveness of the other side.

Every time I sit down at a table and negotiate something, from contract terms to buying a property or a company, I remember the four rules of Tit-for-tat: be well-intentioned, be provocative, be indulgent (or inclined to forgive), and be clear. I am convinced that one of the sources of wealth is the way we relate to the other actors in the market over the long run. The combined value of acting honestly and with integrity, being clear, being nice, striking back at betrayal yet also knowing how to turn the page—all this indicates that we are

---

34 Axelrod, *Evolution of Cooperation*, 54.

35 Axelrod, *Evolution of Cooperation*, 40.

trustworthy and interested in creating reciprocal value. In the end, one of the lessons of Axelrod's experimental tournament and the performance of Tit-for-tat is that greed and a focus on the short run will weaken us in an environment where interactions among parties are frequent and prolonged.

Given all of the above, El Rosario's partners decided to open the bank negotiations in a spirit of conversation and an interest in protecting the relationships with the bank that we had been building since long before the fish-farming company existed. Not with a strategy based on force.

THE SHADOW OF THE FUTURE

Robert Axelrod undermined one of the beliefs that had been associated with "the prisoner's dilemma" for decades: that the most appropriate strategy for an individual is to betray and exploit others. To explain why, he coined a concept called "the shadow of the future."[36]

The shadow of the future is the parties' consciousness that they should cooperate based on the probability of future interactions. If the probability of their interaction recurring in the future is low, then cooperation in the present becomes difficult; the individuals are more likely to be hostile or greedy. But when the relationship will most likely continue over time (because the parties are active in the same industry or because they are associates, friends, family, etc.), the shadow of the future will incentivize mutual cooperation. The reason, according to Axelrod, is that the parties can utilize the threat of retaliation against potential betrayal. And they will be able to follow

---

36 Axelrod, *Evolution of Cooperation*, 124.

through on that threat if the interaction is lasting, if the shadow of the future is long enough.

That is why an important way to promote cooperation is to arrange that the same two individuals will meet each other again, be able to recognize each other from the past, and recall how the other has behaved until now. This continuing interaction stabilizes cooperation.

Human evolution selects those who can cooperate, who are better able to carry out exchanges of mutual value. Reciprocity, not selfishness, is the trait that brings higher rewards in our species. Therefore, I do not see negotiations as a confrontation but as an opportunity to create the greatest possible value with other people.

Life is not zero-sum. For me to do well, things do not have to go badly for others. That idea, rooted in historical beliefs and resentments, frequently blocks our ability to generate wealth. Perhaps one way to change this is to lengthen the shadow of the future—to show that, over the long run, everyone in a market will do better if they cooperate and prioritize mutual benefit.

One of Deepak Malhotra's most useful teachings in his classes is that, in any negotiation, one has to write the victory speech of his or her counterpart.[37] That person sitting across the table—how will they communicate to the world that they "won" in this negotiation? Putting this into practice, we can better articulate what value the other party is bringing to the table, and above all, we can understand that the other's victory is a condition for our own.

In the end, the negotiation with the bank and the partners in El Rosario was as positive as it could be. Everyone took responsibility for the debt, and although we lost money, the

---

37   Malhotra, *Negotiating the Impossible*, 19-20.

bank allowed us to finance our payments so as not to affect our capacity to create value. It was the best way out of a problem that had been building for ten years.

PRIORITIZING RELATIONSHIPS

In March 2018, three of us met with the bank as representatives of all the partners. We brought a presentation that had only ten slides, summarizing the origins of El Rosario, what happened after that, what we learned, and our proposal. We were tense, because we knew the bank held all the legal cards, but we also knew that if they chose to be inflexible, that would draw out the process, which neither they nor we wanted to see.

The meeting began well, and the bank's team seemed sympathetic and receptive, but then one of our partners went off-script. He ended the presentation with a proposal aligned with the faction that had originally wanted a hostile negotiation. Of course, that went nowhere, so we had to ask for a second meeting. Finally, the bank agreed to abrogate the individual responsibility for the collective debt, to reduce the interest payment that was due, and to refinance each partner's share of the debt. That way, the bank would recover what it had lent us, and we could move ahead with closing the book on the fish farm.

Unfortunately, what seemed like good news turned out to be the prelude to the thorniest moment of the story. One of the final agreements we made with the bank said that all the partners would turn over an initial payment a few days after closing the negotiations. We accepted, signed papers, and left with a feeling of satisfaction. But one of the partners closest to me changed his mind the next day, upsetting three-and-a-half months of negotiations.

Although I can usually stay calm, that day I felt defeated

and furious. When this partner called me, I remembered what I had said to the group several times during our conversations, "A year from now, this problem will no longer exist. But the way we behave while we are solving it will be with us for the rest of our lives." That quote from Tim Ferris gave me perspective to see beyond my anger and to hear the explanation my partner gave.

This partner said that his family would not let him accept the bank's condition, and therefore he could not hand over the money. But he told me that he himself would accompany me to renegotiate, that he would take on the responsibility of doing what was needed to rescue the process. I valued his honesty, and together we got through the impasse. Now the problem does not exist, and the way we resolved it brought us closer together.

The opposite happened with two other partners, who first committed to paying the money and later found a way to avoid keeping their word. That problem no longer exists either, but their way of confronting it damaged our relationships.

Despite all these hurdles, on July 4, 2018, the day I turned forty-four, the news I had been awaiting for months finally arrived: the liquidation of El Rosario was complete. I took it as a birthday present, but that was not all. I felt as if I were being handed a PhD that cost me ten years and a lot of money but that left me with priceless lessons. It was only then that I was able to identify the biases from which I led the company.

CHAPTER 8

IDENTIFY YOUR BIASES

Looking back, it is easy to explain El Rosario's defects: we were overconfident in our abilities. We thought we understood, rationally, why something was not working, and so we made decisions to compensate for that particular flaw. This ease in justifying our interventions kept us from seeing what we did not want to see: that we could neither predict nor control what was going on. We were facing an absolutely uncertain future, but we did not want to accept that.

There is an entire market of academics and journalists devoted to explaining why such-and-such had to happen—even if, before the event, they said it was impossible. The book you are reading is a clear example: I am suggesting hypotheses to explain the failure of El Rosario, as if everything that happened made sense in a way I can now see easily. Yet I know that is more of an illusion than a reality. As statistician Nassim Taleb says:[38]

---

38 Nassim Nicholas Taleb, *The Black Swan: The Impact of the Highly Improbable* (Random House, 2007), 12.

Events present themselves to us in a distorted way. Consider the nature of information: of the millions, maybe even trillions, of small facts that prevail before an event occurs, only a few will turn out to be relevant later to your understanding of what happened. Because your memory is limited and filtered, you will be inclined to remember those data that subsequently match the facts.

Hindsight bias is the tendency to perceive events of the past as if they had been predictable, as if they could not have occurred any other way. This is one of the central biases covered in *Thinking, Fast and Slow*. Daniel Kahneman writes:[39]

The idea that the future is unpredictable is undermined every day by the ease with which the past is explained...Everything makes sense in hindsight, a fact that financial pundits exploit every evening as they offer convincing accounts of the day's events. And we cannot suppress the powerful intuition that what makes sense in hindsight today was predictable yesterday. The illusion that we understand the past fosters overconfidence in our ability to predict the future.

It is a vicious circle. The more confidence we have that we can explain past events, the more we believe we can predict the future, and this prejudice can interfere with the goal of creating value.

As of this writing, almost two hundred cognitive biases have been identified. Evidence suggests that it is impossible to eradicate biases in our thinking, but if we are aware of them and can identify those to which we are most vulnerable, we

---

39   Daniel Kahneman, *Thinking, Fast and Slow* (Farrar, Straus and Giroux, 2011), 218.

can spot them in time to keep the damage under control. So, in this chapter I will try to describe some of the other biases that influenced my decisions as the chairman of El Rosario. These are common biases in the business environment, so becoming conscious of them is an exercise in responsibility and self-protection.

As entrepreneurs and executives, we experience daily what Nassim Taleb has called "the practice of uncertainty."[40] There is a lot we do not know, and there is not a map or model that guarantees success or the creation of value. However, understanding logical traps can be useful in ensuring that our practice of uncertainty—of dealing with the unknown—does not get waylaid by errors we already know well.

UNDERSTANDING LOGICAL TRAPS

In *Thinking, Fast and Slow*, psychologist Daniel Kahneman sums up his findings about how human beings make decisions. The book, published in 2011, a decade after Kahneman won a Nobel Prize, argues that our brain thinks via two parallel systems. System 1 is rapid and intuitive; System 2, slower and more analytical.[41]

System 1 allows for making quick judgments, like recognizing irony in a statement or identifying patterns in a data set without deep analysis. System 2 involves critical thinking, evaluating a situation according to its many variables, carefully thinking through each one of those, and reaching conclusions after a meticulous process. The latter is a system that demands more mental effort, of the sort we generally use to make a cost-

---

40 Taleb, *The Black Swan*, xxvi.

41 Kahneman, *Thinking*, 20.

benefit analysis, to devise financial projections, or to investigate a market.

Kahneman (and his colleague Amos Tversky) base their approach on heuristics, mental shortcuts or quick associations that the mind uses to simplify the process of making and evaluating decisions.[42] Heuristics are efficient, unconscious strategies that we use to estimate the probability of an uncertain event. For example, when we meet new people, we do not sit down and make lists of their characteristics before deciding whether or not to trust them; our judgments occur almost immediately. Or, when faced with various alternatives for the new logo of a company, there may be one that strikes us as most attractive, even before we come up with any reasons to justify that preference.

Kahneman and Tversky assert that heuristics occur naturally and are not irrational; they result from very sophisticated mental processes. Nonetheless, because they work so quickly, the heuristics of System 1 are very susceptible to deviating from logic and from the laws of probability. Although extremely useful, they frequently lead to systematic errors of thinking, or cognitive biases. Many of these prejudices are obstacles to creating value.

In an ideal world, an executive would always make decisions by employing System 2—reviewing as many variables as possible without rush. But it is naive to take that as the reality of the business world. In my experience, both systems are necessary: System 2 because of everything I have described in the chapter on mathematical thinking, and System 1 because it helps us read circumstances with agility and intuition.

Some studies show that how much an individual will strive

---

42   Kahneman, *Thinking*, 8–12.

to judge situations via System 2 depends on his or her motivation and how important he or she judges the matter at hand to be. Still, there is sufficient evidence that it is impossible to eliminate all biases. We can mitigate their impact, but we cannot think without them.

In *Heuristics and Biases: The Psychology of Intuitive Judgment*, a fundamental book for understanding the science behind heuristics and biases, Thomas Gilovich and Dale Griffin summarize it this way:[43]

> An associationist, parallel-processing system ("System 1") that renders quick, holistic judgments is always in operation—not just when motivation is low and judgments are made on the cheap. The assessments made by the associationist system are then supplemented—and sometimes overridden—by the output of a more deliberate, serial, and rule-based system ("System 2").

I will go on to describe four biases that El Rosario introduced me to. These biases are now on my radar so that, in the future, I can identify them in time to quickly escape from their traps.

ESCALATING COMMITMENT BIAS

At El Rosario, we fell into the escalating commitment bias. The Decision Lab summarizes the bias this way: "our tendency to remain committed to our past behaviors, particularly

---

43   Thomas Gilovich and Dale Griffin, "Introduction—Heuristics and Biases: Then and Now," in *Heuristics and Biases: The Psychology of Intuitive Judgment*, ed. Thomas Gilovich, Dale Griffin, and Daniel Kahneman (Cambridge University Press, 2002), 16.

those exhibited publicly, even if they do not have desirable outcomes."[44]

We invested in a business that rapidly revealed itself as unviable. It was limited by structural issues over which we had no control—the geographic location of the plant, the deforestation upstream, the social and labor conditions of the area, the ecological importance of the river, etc. In 2016, when no outside investor wanted to become a partner in the company because it had no net value after five years of operation, our most rational decision would have been to liquidate, pay off our debts, and give up the effort. But we did the opposite. Escalating commitment bias led us to invest still more of our own capital, probably because we did not want to admit that ten successful businessmen could fail. In order to stay consistent with our public images, our pasts, our track records and reputations, we made a decision that ended up being more costly.

In *The Art of Thinking Clearly*, Swiss writer Rolf Dobelli discusses more than eighty biases, including a derivative of the escalating commitment bias called the "sunk cost fallacy." Here is how he describes this fallacy:[45]

> The sunk cost fallacy is most dangerous when we have invested a lot of time, money, energy, or love in something. This investment becomes a reason to carry on, even if we are dealing with a lost cause. The more we invest, the greater the sunk costs are, and the greater the urge to continue becomes... Rational decision-making requires you to forget about the costs incurred to date. No matter how much you have already

---

44   Dan Pilat and Sekoul Krastev, "Why Do People Support Their Past Ideas, Even When Presented with Evidence That They're Wrong?," The Decision Lab, accessed September 10, 2024, https://thedecisionlab.com/biases/commitment-bias.

45   Rolf Dobelli, *The Art of Thinking Clearly* (Sceptre, 2013), 18–19.

invested, only your assessment of the future costs and benefits counts.

He connects it with the escalating commitment bias this way:[46]

> This irrational behavior is driven by a need for consistency. After all, consistency signifies credibility. We find contradictions abominable. If we decide to cancel a project halfway through, we create a contradiction: We admit that we once thought differently. Carrying on with a meaningless project delays this painful realisation and keeps up appearances.

This error is systematic. Years after the failure of the tilapia farm, I keep running into it. Often, when I face a crisis, the thought that automatically comes to mind is that surely an injection of capital will do the job.

I have found this way of thinking common among executives with whom I work and entrepreneurs in whose projects I invest—the notion that problems can be solved with more investment, with a financial life preserver to carry the company to shore. And, indeed, sometimes this is true. There are very successful companies that were once on the point of disappearing before receiving an injection of capital. But most of the time, that is not how it works. Most of the time, the solution is not to invest more but to study the reasons why a company is still not creating or capturing sufficient value.

In such situations, the best thing to do is interrupt the first way of thinking and activate System 2: ask difficult questions, review variables, and be ready to make uncomfortable decisions.

---

46   Dobelli, *Art of Thinking*, 18.

A red flag signaling the presence of this bias is when the heads of a company seek to move obstacles out of the way by using the lever of finance—more money—rather than showing the curiosity to first review the possible structural causes of their problems.

THE OVERCONFIDENCE EFFECT

In his book *The Black Swan*, Nassim Taleb explores human beings' relationship with uncertainty and our ways of hiding the fact that we know less than we think we do.[47] Overconfidence in our knowledge is one of the most common biases. To demonstrate how common it is, Taleb proposes an exercise for groups of any size:

Ask each person in the room to independently estimate a range of possible values for a number set in such a way that they believe that they have a 98 percent chance of being right, and less than 2 percent chance of being wrong. In other words, whatever they are guessing has about a 2 percent chance to fall outside their range. For example:

- "I am 98 percent confident that the population of Rajasthan is between 15 and 23 million."
- "I am 98 percent confident that Catherine II of Russia had between 34 and 63 lovers."

Note that the subjects (your victims) are free to set their range as wide as they want: you are not trying to gauge their knowledge but rather their evaluation of their own knowledge.

This exercise is based on an experiment designed by pro-

---

47   Taleb, *The Black Swan*, 145.

fessors Marc Alpert and Howard Raiffa. Their results were surprising: nearly half of their sample (45 percent) did not come up with correct estimates. That is, they overestimated their knowledge, falling into the 2 percent probability of being wrong.[48]

Most of us think we know more than we really do. This overconfidence leads to problematic decisions, predictions, and behaviors. The experiment I have just noted is not intended to measure whether people's estimates about an event are correct or not but to indicate how far their real knowledge of a subject falls short of what they think they know.

Ironically, those who consider themselves "experts" in something are more susceptible to fall into this bias. An economics professor and a plumber know the same amount about what the price of a gallon of gas will be two years from now, but the professor will hazard a guess more confidently.

Perhaps this too happened to us at El Rosario. The fact that almost all the partners had experience in the agricultural and techno-industrial sector made us more likely to look at our company overconfidently. What could go wrong, given how much accumulated experience we had? We began by overestimating our abilities. Thereafter, every decision we made rejected the possibility that we might be wrong or that we might lack the skills and resources to make a fish farm succeed.

In fact, the more we know, the more we should recognize how complicated and unpredictable the future is. Taleb says: "The gains in our ability to model (and predict) the world may be

48   Marc Alpert and Howard Raiffa, "21—A Progress Report on the Training of Probability Assessors," in *Judgement Under Uncertainty: Heuristics and Biases*, ed. Daniel Kahneman, Paul Slovic, and Amos Tversky (Cambridge University Press, 1982), 294–305, https://doi.org/10.1017/CBO9780511809477.022.

dwarfed by the increases in its complexity—implying a greater and greater role for the unpredicted."[49]

His book is revealing because it is an alarm bell for any of us who believe that with strategic planning, studies of consumption, financial projections, etc., we can predict the future of a company or a product. In place of such overconfidence, Taleb advocates permanent humility and curiosity, and a special sort of attention to identify, in the moment, what can be an opportunity to shape history:[50]

> The strategy for the discoverers and entrepreneurs is to rely less on top-down planning and focus on maximum tinkering and recognizing opportunities when they present themselves. So I disagree with the followers of Marx and those of Adam Smith: the reason free markets work is because they allow people to be lucky, thanks to aggressive trial and error, not by giving rewards or "incentives" for skill.

UPSIDE VS. DOWNSIDE

Cognitive biases tend to assign more importance to a business's upside (potential profits) than to its downside (the losses it could generate). One of the mantras of business schools and popular wisdom is: the greater the risk, the higher the return. This is supposed to be a linear relationship, and we make decisions on that basis. But I do not take it for an absolute truth. There are many opportunities where there are asymmetries: businesses that have a high upside and a low downside.

The case of El Rosario was the opposite. The upside was

---

49   Taleb, *The Black Swan*, 136.

50   Taleb, *The Black Swan*, xxi.

generating value for the partners, making a contribution to regional development, and creating jobs for people who had few such options. We never calculated the downside, so it surprised us when we found ourselves pressured by the large investment we had made.

The downside of El Rosario was easy to identify, but all of us missed it. In Colombia, an actor can be in compliance with all environmental regulations, but if at some point it is demonstrated that the actor has caused environmental damage, he or she faces criminal charges with no statute of limitations. This makes sense to me. That level of consciousness about respecting and protecting nature is more and more the spirit of our times. Still, it meant a company like the fish farm, which was having a permanent effect on the natural ecosystem, was much more vulnerable to being accused (and convicted) of damage to the environment. The potential upside of the business could not in any way compensate for that downside.

Perhaps expert advice on environmental law, or even just the common sense of one of the partners, would have been enough to make us take a closer look at the decision to create an industrial plant of that scale in such a diverse and important ecosystem.

In psychological terms, the upside vs. downside bias is a manifestation of the bias of optimism and of the "planning fallacy." In a 2003 article, Daniel Kahneman and professor Dan Lovallo described that fallacy:[51]

---

51   Dan Lovallo and Daniel Kahneman, "Delusions of Success: How Optimism Undermines Executives' Decisions," *Harvard Business Review*, July 2003, https://hbr.org/2003/07/delusions-of-success-how-optimism-undermines-executives-decisions.

We don't believe that the high number of business failures is best explained as the result of rational choices gone wrong. Rather, we see it as a consequence of flawed decision making. When forecasting the outcomes of risky projects, executives all too easily fall victim to what psychologists call the planning fallacy. In its grip, managers make decisions based on delusional optimism rather than on a rational weighting of gains, losses, and probabilities. They overestimate benefits and underestimate costs.

The excess of optimism, which the authors call "seeing through rose-colored glasses," can be explained by cognitive biases and organizational pressures. It can be attributed to limits of the human imagination. As Lovallo and Kahneman write in the same article:[52]

No matter how detailed, the business scenarios used in planning are generally inadequate. The reason is simple: Any complex project is subject to myriad problems—from technology failures to shifts in exchange rates to bad weather—and it is beyond the reach of the human imagination to foresee all of them at the outset. As a result, scenario planning can seriously understate the probability of things going awry.

I am not saying we need to be pessimists. Optimism bolsters our spirits when pursuing opportunities in uncertain scenarios becomes difficult. However, it is important to qualify our optimism and establish some systems for maintaining a balance, so as to try to avoid making decisions that lead to catastrophic downsides. Kahneman and Lovallo recommend being disci-

---

52   Lovallo and Kahneman, "Delusions of Success."

plined in scrutinizing our assumptions, inviting those with outside perspectives to examine our plans, and recognizing that the future is uncertain and not necessarily rosy.

TAKING AN OUTSIDE VIEW

Perhaps the most useful tool when it comes to making business projections is taking an outside view. The inside view is that of the partners in a business, who make forecasts based on the data they have at hand: the company's mission, resources, experience, etc. From that information they construct possible scenarios, which tend to be exaggeratedly optimistic. In contrast, the outside view ignores the specific details of a business; instead of making forecasts, it compares the business to other similar companies. According to the authors, this view is usually more accurate.

Evidently, all the decisions we made at El Rosario stemmed from an inside view, and probably this made us more susceptible to exaggerating the upside and underestimating the downside. That said, it was hard to find examples of aquaculture companies similar to ours because the majority were in other provinces of the country, in very different environments. There was little data from which to construct an outside view that could have tamped down the optimism in our forecasts and decisions.

It would be naive to think we can eliminate biases through willpower; because humans do not make decisions based solely on logic, biases are inevitable. However, you can discern the right moment to use the parallel systems we discussed earlier, applying your intuition or analysis as needed. Perhaps then you can avoid the depression I fell into after El Rosario was liquidated.

CONCLUSION

Three years after we liquidated El Rosario, I went on a fishing trip with my father, my brother, and some friends along the rivers of the state of Vichada in Colombia's eastern lowlands. In the past, these trips had been restorative, giving me the energy and perspective I needed to manage my business and familial responsibilities. But this time was different. As soon as I got there, I felt the river pulling on me. I sank into deep sadness.

For a week, from sunrise to sunset, I cried silently, hiding the tears behind my dark glasses so the others would not see. I did not fish much, did not enjoy the landscape, did not participate in conversations at all. Without knowing how, I slid into an abyss that felt like the onset of death.

On my way back to Medellín, I called my wife to let her know how bad I was feeling. I was on the verge of being hospitalized. Suddenly, without any warning, I was face to face with one of my worst fears: losing the ability to work. Diagnosed with depression, I began a long course of treatment to overcome the sadness and apathy whose source I did not know.

At that time in my life, I should have been able to list many reasons for feeling satisfied: my daughters and friends, a fantastic team at work, economic prosperity, and a growing company where I could freely experiment and create. Yet I felt a vise clamping me to darkness. It was a terrible feeling. Not even during the worst times of El Rosario, when I was exhausted and pessimistic, when I had to devote almost all my energy to that failing company, had I faced that kind of threat—a force that paralyzed my inclination to find value in whatever fate threw my way.

Normally, I can deal with whatever comes. Challenges interest me, and I find it intellectually enjoyable to turn things around, to think up strategies for converting difficulties into possibilities. I like uncertainty, and I feel my batteries recharging when I sense an opportunity. But when this depression hit, that attitude disappeared. Eventually, I began to understand that the depression was the manifestation of a lack of self-care that had been building up for years. I saw that the seeds of this darkness had been planted long before I could feel its effects.

At first, I saw my depression as a dirty trick played by destiny, a kind of punishment. Now, without declaring victory, I understand it as a spiritual emergency: painful, but clarifying in the end. Through the Unique Ability™, which I mentioned in Chapter 3, I found that I devote only 20 percent of my time to the activities I am exceptional at, even though those are the only ones we do with passion and energy and at which we continue to get better. Most things I do every day are ones that I am less competent in, that arouse no passion in me and can, on the other hand, generate conflicts, a sense of failure, and stress.

It is paradoxical, but in order to live out the goal of creating value for others, we have to put ourselves first. Without routines of self-care and reflection, the entrepreneurial life—in which we have to give so much to others—can become suffocating.

But the opposite is also true: the entrepreneurial life, if lived with wisdom, can be a practice full of meaning and fulfillment.

The Unique Ability program showed me that I needed to devote most of my time and energy to the daily actions I know how to do best. I can delegate the rest to people who have more ability to move them along. This is a kind of self-care that also nurtures organizational value and talent.

If you lead a company that is both valuable and profitable, it is easy to get distracted from your goals and to settle instead into the privileges of status. Economic "success" and the approval of others may bring the illusion of being already a finished product, which leads to the risk of identifying only as a businessperson and all that implies. This can lead to neglecting the many other identities that make us up—citizen, child, parent, reader, learner—which also, inevitably, contribute to our capacity to generate value for the world.

Mental health disorders are signs showing the need to integrate parts of ourselves that have been left unattended. My "failure" at El Rosario and my depression, for example, have been lessons in humility. They have opened a rocky road toward understanding that nothing is worth more than this ephemeral existence and that businesses are just one of the means of getting to know ourselves and other people better. To find others and exchange talents. If I have learned anything from those difficult experiences, it is that wealth is fragile and, as with our spirits, we must care for and cultivate it at all times.

It is no accident that the fundamental tenet of many religions and disciplines is "do no harm." I think that the principle of companies with integrity is the same, and the place to start practicing that principle is with oneself. When life in a business starts to wear down your health or the health of those who work there, pause, look within, and retrace your steps so you can get back to creating value while maintaining everyone's well-being; otherwise, you may feel like you are fishing in the sand.

WHEN TO RESUME

Five years have gone by between the liquidation of Piscícola El Rosario and the writing of this book. What at the time seemed a catastrophe that threatened the stability of Iluma (and what my family and thousands of people had built over four decades) I now see as an indispensable lesson in the infinite game of creating value through business. Without my depression, I would not have the incessant contemplation—what the stoics called prosoche—to reflect on what El Rosario taught me. Without everything El Rosario taught me, I would not have had the tools to contribute in a more conscious and effective way to the growth of Iluma.

Now that I have resumed operations with more awareness than before, I would like to share the equation that guides my decisions and those of around a thousand beating hearts who, alongside me, invest a part of their lives in our project of nourishing the world. It is, essentially, a condensed version of what I have shared in this book.

The first part of the equation is the human element. Life is everyone's most important asset, the asset we most need to take care of and the one we devote the most thought to. At Iluma, we do not take lightly the fact that our system is sustained by the time, effort, and knowledge of hundreds of human beings who want to devote parts of their lives to better nourish the world.

The human element has one main multiplier: mindset. The belief system that connects us as an organization has five key principles:

- **Consciousness of the goal:** Our purpose is our horizon. We want to nourish the world better, so every action that each of us takes is guided by that purpose. Consciousness of a goal is a multiplier principle because it expands possibilities and helps us take risks, experiment, and explore the countless ways that our purpose can be realized.
- **Autonomy:** We do not believe in companies that insist on controlling and dictating what people should do and what they should not. We have complete trust in our team because we recognize that each individual is the master or his or her fate. We provide incentives for autonomy, regulated by the awareness that we are part of a system that in turn makes us interdependent. Personal responsibility is fundamental to cooperation among all. We try to create a safe and supportive environment in which everyone gives their best and, at the same time, knows they can count on the best of others to meet daily challenges.
- **Curiosity:** To stay relevant, we need an attitude of permanent curiosity, of cultivating individual wealth and the wealth of the system through knowledge, intellect, productive capacity, and empathy. By identifying opportunities and taking advantage of them, curiosity has allowed our business to constantly develop new capabilities. Though it is infinite, such curiosity cannot be taken for granted. It is something that we encourage and practice in daily conversation—asking, discovering, suggesting.
- **Teamwork:** Teamwork stems from the recognition, arrived at with vulnerability and humility, that we as individuals are not finished products. Acting from the certainty of being connected with hundreds of souls who share the same goal is an engine of celebration and joy. If we cooperate and take

full advantage of being a network, then each person's impact is amplified.

- **Generating value:** We create the greatest possible value in everything we do for our customers, for society, and for the other members of our team. We want to be expansive actors, people who connect with the needs around us, who offer valuable solutions, and who then capture a part of that value-add.

Those five principles are framed by a practice that defines us, as I mentioned in Chapter 6: Organizations, families, cities, individuals—all are defined by how they talk and what they talk about. It is in conversation that reality starts to be transformed; that is where an idea is nourished, structured, grows, and expands. Therefore, we at Iluma are very conscious of the importance of conversation in developing a growth mindset.

To best amplify the human element of business, we opt for a culture of innovation, simplicity, and permanent learning. We are on an endless path, in constant evolution, and we believe that a diverse collection of human beings connected to the same goal, multiplied by a mentality of abundance, is a catalyst for knowledge and value.

We are an organization that seeks to have global importance not from exploitation of the planet, or from selling cheap products, or from employing cheap labor but from our ability to engage in unique thinking. We want to be known for making use of our strengths in technology, knowledge, and innovation so as to compete with the world's best. We are, in principle, an intellectual property organization, one that makes use of those three factors to bring exceptional and distinct value to our customers. Those customers are truly the protagonists of our story.

Finally, we have Innovation Labs, where we allow ourselves to create new things without knowing whether or not they will work. We start small, we build prototypes, and we create a Minimal Viable Product before taking it large-scale and into a market. This is a space for permanent conversation and experimentation, supported by an internal network and outside allies (scholars and scientists) who contribute their experience, knowledge, and abilities. Together, we are able to accelerate our processes and design solutions that generate a more significant impact.

WHY WE WORK

As of December 2024, Iluma Alliance is impacting more than 500 million people in the world. Every day, the work of every one of the beating hearts making up Iluma has an impact: their abilities are out there, their intellects are out there, their lives are out there. Our goal is that, from this ecosystem, this alliance, we will succeed in impacting a billion people by 2030—one-eighth of humanity. Whether we succeed or not, whether we reach that figure ahead of time or take longer than we plan, what matters to us is that the alliance is a platform for the growth of those who work within it and a source of nourishment for millions of people worldwide. That way, they too can contribute to a better-nourished and more prosperous world.

What change do you want to see in the world, and how can your work contribute to that vision? If you had unlimited resources, what problem would you solve first? How can you start addressing that problem now, even on a small scale? How do you want people to feel after interacting with you or with your company? What legacy do you want to leave as a leader?

Remember, small, daily actions either align you with your purpose or distance you from it. I hope that after reading my story, you feel empowered to learn from your mistakes, recommit to your values, and leverage your strengths and unique perspective. Like this one, your story will not end with failure as long as you are dedicated to doing better for yourself, your company, your community, your industry, and the world.

I wish you the best on your journey.

ADDITIONAL RESOURCES

If you are looking to expand your understanding of the topics I just discussed, I highly recommend these online courses, podcasts, apps, and books.

Mathematical Thinking:

- Introduction to Mathematical Thinking —Coursera
- Terence Tao Teaches Mathematical Thinking—MasterClass
- The Foundations Are Math and Logic—Naval Ravikant
- Math | Riddles and Puzzles—App for iOS
- *The Joy of X: A Guided Tour of Math, from One to Infinity*— Steven Strogatz
- *How Not to Be Wrong: The Power of Mathematical Thinking*— Jordan Ellenberg
- *Thinking in Systems*—Donella H. Meadows

Mindset:

- *Mindset: The New Psychology of Success*—Carol S. Dweck

- *The Laws of Lifetime Growth: Always Make Your Future Bigger Than Your Past*—Dan Sullivan and Catherine Nomura
- *Antifragile: Things That Gain from Disorder*—Nassim Nicholas Taleb
- *The Future Is Faster Than You Think: How Converging Technologies Are Transforming Business, Industries, and Our Lives*—Peter H. Diamandis, and Steven Kotler
- *Tools of Titans: The Tactics, Routines, and Habits of Billionaires, Icons, and World-Class Performers*—Tim Ferriss

Biases:

- *Thinking, Fast and Slow*—Daniel Kahneman
- *The Black Swan: The Impact of the Highly Improbable*—Nassim Nicholas Taleb
- *The Art of Thinking Clearly*—Rolf Dobelli
- *Heuristics and Biases: The Psychology of Intuitive Judgment*—Thomas Gilovich, Dale Griffin, and Daniel Kahneman (editors)
- *Blink: The Power of Thinking Without Thinking*—Malcolm Gladwell
- *Delusions of Success: How Optimism Undermines Executives' Decisions*—Dan Lovallo and Daniel Kahneman

Spirituality:

- *The Information: A History, a Theory, a Flood*—James Gleick
- *The Almanack of Naval Ravikant: A Guide to Wealth and Happiness*—Eric Jorgenson
- *How Innovation Works: And Why It Flourishes in Freedom*—Matt Ridley

- *The Origins of Virtue: Human Instincts and the Evolution of Cooperation*—Matt Ridley
- *The Evolution of Cooperation*—Robert Axelrod
- *Influence: The Psychology of Persuasion*—Robert B. Cialdini
- *Antifragile: Things That Gain from Disorder*—Nassim Nicholas Taleb
- *La Estrategia Emergente*—Alejandro Salazar
- *Reclaiming Conversation: The Power of Talk in a Digital Age*—Sherry Turkle

ABOUT THE AUTHOR

ALEJANDRO MESA GÓMEZ is a business leader and entrepreneur on a mission to create a better-nourished world. His career has taken him from roles at Premex and Schering Plough Corporation to founding and growing companies across the agribusiness, food, biotechnology, and analytics sectors. Now, as the CEO of Iluma Alliance, he leads a diverse team of around a thousand passionate individuals dedicated to improving nutrition through mindset, knowledge, technology, life sciences, and innovation.

Building on a multidisciplinary education spanning agronomy, agricultural economics, and business administration, Alejandro has honed his skills through executive programs at prestigious institutions like Harvard, Stanford, Columbia, and Singularity University. A self-described mindset farmer and compulsive book buyer, he believes in the power of intent and continuously seeks opportunities to learn and evolve. He loves exploring diverse fields such as biohacking, strategy, game theory, analytics, biotech, and neuroscience to better understand himself and the world around him.

Alejandro cherishes his role as a father to his three daughters, who inspire him to lead by example and make a lasting impact. To this end, he creates value and contributes his expertise through collaborative board memberships.

In *Fishing the Unexpected: Navigating the Unpredictable Waters of Entrepreneurship*, Alejandro shares invaluable lessons learned from his successes and failures, offering readers a candid and insightful look into the mind of a purpose-driven leader. Offering a good balance of wisdom, wit, and humility, this book is a must-read for anyone seeking to navigate the complexities of business while staying true to their values and making a positive difference in the world.

www.ingramcontent.com/pod-product-compliance
Lightning Source LLC
Chambersburg PA
CBHW030526210326
41597CB00013B/1047